乐贸LEMO
LOVE · EASY · MONEY · OPEN
·跟着老外学外贸系列·

WE HAVE A

优势成交

老外这样做销售（第二版）

［摩洛哥］ Abdelhak Benkerroum（阿道） 著
范文曲 译

DEAL 2

中国海关出版社有限公司
·北京·

图书在版编目（CIP）数据

优势成交：老外这样做销售/（摩洛哥）阿道（Abdelhak Benkerroum）著；范文曲翻译．—2 版．—北京：中国海关出版社有限公司，2019.10

ISBN 978-7-5175-0370-5

Ⅰ．①优… Ⅱ．①阿… ②范… Ⅲ．①市场营销 Ⅳ．①F713.3

中国版本图书馆 CIP 数据核字（2019）第 146153 号

著作权合同登记号
图字：01－2017－6064

优势成交：老外这样做销售（第二版）

YOUSHI CHENGJIAO：LAOWAI ZHEYANG ZUO XIAOSHOU（DI－ER BAN）

作　　者：（摩洛哥）Abdelhak Benkerroum（阿道）
译　　者：范文曲
策划编辑：马　超
责任编辑：郭　坤
责任监制：郭　坤　赵　宇
出版发行：中国海关出版社有限公司
社　　址：北京市朝阳区东四环南路甲 1 号　　邮政编码：100023
网　　址：www.hgcbs.com.cn；www.hgbookvip.com
编 辑 部：01065194242－7585（电话）　　01065194234（传真）
发 行 部：01065194221/4238/4246/4227（电话）　　01065194233（传真）
社办书店：01065195616/5127（电话/传真）　　01065194262/63（邮购电话）
印　　刷：北京铭成印刷有限公司　　经　　销：新华书店
开　　本：710mm×1000mm　1/16
印　　张：16　　字　　数：275 千字
版　　次：2019 年 10 月第 2 版
印　　次：2019 年 10 月第 1 次印刷
书　　号：ISBN　978－7－5175－0370－5
定　　价：58.00 元

序言

三个儿子与 17 头骆驼

有个阿拉伯人把 17 头骆驼作为遗产留给了他的三个儿子。在他去世后，他的儿子们聚在一起打开了遗嘱。

遗嘱上写着："我有 17 头骆驼，三个儿子。大儿子将得到一半数量的骆驼，二儿子得到总数三分之一的骆驼，最小的儿子得到总数九分之一的骆驼。"

三个儿子疑惑不解。要怎样按照遗嘱里说的来分 17 头骆驼呢？怎么可能把 17 头骆驼等分成两份、三份或九份呢？于是三个儿子开始商量如何在不杀死骆驼的情况下公平地进行分配。正当三兄弟的讨论逐渐升温时，一位骑着骆驼的阿拉伯老人顺道路过。他下了骆驼，表示愿意帮助他们。他看过遗嘱后思索了一番，说道："我把我的骆驼借给你们，那么你们三个就有 18 头骆驼（17+1=18）了，现在我们就按遗嘱上说的分一分。

大儿子得到 9 头骆驼（1/2 × 18=9）；

二儿子得到 6 头骆驼（1/3 × 18=6）；

小儿子得到 2 头骆驼（1/9 × 18=2）。

如此一来你们分到的骆驼的总数为 17 头（9+6+2=17）。剩下的 1 头骆驼是我的，我将其取回。"

然后他便骑上自己的骆驼离开了。

Preface

Three Sons and 17 Camels

An Arab man left 17 camels as an asset for his three sons. When he passed away, his sons got together and opened the Will.

The Will stated: "I have 17 camels, and I have three sons. Divide my camels in such a way that my eldest son gets half of them, the second one gets 1/3 of the total and my youngest son gets 1/9 of the total number of camels."

The three sons were stunned. How to divide 17 camels as mentioned in the Will? It is impossible to divide 17 into half, or 17 by 3, or 17 by 9. So the sons started negotiating on how to divide them equally, without killing any camel. As the discussion heated up, an old Arab riding a camel goes riding by. He stopped, got off his camel, and proposed to help. He read the Will, pondered over it for some moment, then said: "I will lend my camel to you, which makes the three of you owners of 18 camels (17+1=18). Now let's divide as per this Will.

The eldest son gets 1/2 of 18 = 9

The second one gets 1/3 of 18 = 6

The youngest gets 1/9 of 18 = 2

Now the total number of camels is 17 (9+6+2=17). There is 1 camel left, and it is mine, so I will take it back."

He then jumped back on his camel and left.

What does this fascinating story tell us? It first tells us that **there is no problem that can not be solved**. You can look at ANY issue you are facing

这个神奇的故事告诉我们什么？首先，**没有解决不了的问题**。无论你在工作或者生活中遇到任何问题，都要相信会有解决的方法。有些时候只需换个角度看问题，我们就能够找到一个全新的解决方案。这个故事也告诉我们，达成共识或是促成一个交易并非我们所想的那样艰难。拥有正确的态度，谈判各方都可以促成一次成功的谈判。

关键问题：永远要找寻第 18 只骆驼。

任何交易都由 3 个因素组成：人员（People）、产品（Products）以及流程（Processes）。这些因素被简称为 3P。

一个公司或公司内部的一个部门要想存活并持续发展，就需要完全掌控这 3 个要素。

一个拥有好**产品**和好**员工**的公司不知道该干什么，是因为它没有清晰明确地规划**流程**。

一个拥有好**流程**和好**员工**的公司什么都卖不出去，是因为它没有一个好的**产品**。

一个有卓越**产品**和合理化**流程**的公司成不了大事，是因为它的**员工**不够称职。

回首我的职业生涯，我也遇到过在这 3 个因素中缺失了两个却依然存活下来的公司。没错，也许凭一些运气或充足的资金（或两者兼备），那个公司能够存活，但它永远无法发展壮大。一旦市场上有强大的新生竞争者出现，该公司就会迅速被后来者的迅猛之势碾压，其黄金时代也将不复存在。在那时的市场环境下，这样的公司想要转型十分困难。一场金融危机甚至可以在公司意识到市场状况之前就将其彻底摧毁。

《优势成交：老外这样做销售（第二版）》一书选取这 3 个因素中的“人员”和“流程”进行讲述，旨在介绍销售部门内部的逻辑关系。在第一部分，本

at work or in your life, and be sure that there is somehow a way to make it work. Sometimes, just changing the angle from which we view things can expose a whole new world of solutions. This story also tells us that reaching an agreement and striking a deal is not as difficult as we might think. With the right attitude, each party involved in a negotiation can and has to contribute in the success of a negotiation.

Bottom line: Always look for the 18th camel.

Every business is also a combination of three things: People, Products and Processes. These are called the 3P's. In order for a company or a department within the company to survive and thrive, it needs to have full control of all these three variables—all of them.

A company with good **Products** and good **People** will not know what it is doing without clear and documented **Processes**.

A company with good **Processes** and good **People** will never sell anything if it has a bad **Product**.

A company with an exceptional **Product** and streamlined **Processes** will not go anywhere if its **People** are incompetent.

Over the course of my career, I came across companies where two of the three variables were deficient, yet the company managed to survive. Yes, with a bit of luck or a lot of money (or both), that company can still survive, but it will never grow. It will survive only up until the time when a strong new competitor rolls into the market with full speed and full resources, and shows them that the golden days are over. It will also be vulnerable to changes in market conditions. An economic crisis could wipe out companies before they even realize what exactly is going on in the market.

We Have a Deal (Second Edition)*!* is mainly talking about the first P: People, and the last P: Processes. It aims at introducing logical relationship of sales departments. In its first part, it exposes in a very simple and practical manner how a salesman should negotiate for win-win deals, from the moment he starts preparing

书以极为简单实用的方式揭示了作为一名销售人员所应具备的“双赢”谈判技巧，涵盖从开始准备商务会面，到最终成交所涉及的各个方面，并将明确地告诉你说什么和怎么说。在第二部分，本书会阐述如何招聘、考核、维护以及培训销售人员等。第三部分，包含了我个人在与中国销售人员打交道过程中的一些观察。

本书还将解答一些大家关心的问题，如为什么用整数标价不是一个好主意？为什么在有些情况下应该避免争取大客户？如何以及何时在谈判过程中报价？如何回应潜在客户“太贵了”的质疑？

本书是我在世界各地，开展多年跨国合作所得的经验结晶。通过对这些经验的学习，公司可以提升业绩，并获得培训员工的方法，从而培养出出色的谈判者和交易专家。

本书的出版也源于我内心的一种失望。我曾经看到许多培训公司收取极高的费用来培训中国或其他国家公司中的销售团队，告诉销售人员如何销售和谈判。然而，许多这样的培训都只培训销售流程和销售态度。这些培训公司往往在培训中派出励志演讲人，而非引导师或培训师。甚至连培训的标题都令人匪夷所思，比如“一个月内让你的销售业绩提升 35%”或者“88% 的销售代表在此培训后获得了杰出的销售业绩”。我并不排斥励志演讲人，但是在当前的大环境下，一家公司最需要做的是帮助他们的员工掌握相关技能和工具从而赢得市场。这本书的低定价是为了让中国的每一位销售人员都能够有机会阅读并从中获益。我希望本书能够服务并帮助中国的商业公司及企业家在国内外市场上获得成功。

阿 道

宁波东方海默信息咨询有限公司

for the sales meeting, to the moment the deal is closed. It tells you exactly what you have to say and how to say it. In the second part, it explains how to hire, assess, retain, and coach salespeople. In the last part, it relates a few observations from my personal experience dealing with salespeople in China.

This book can answer your questions such as: Why pricing at a round number is a bad idea? Why should I sometimes avoid going after large customers? How and when to announce the price during a negotiation? What to answer when a prospect tells me that my price is too high?

This book is the result of several years I spent working around the world in and with multinationals to drive their business growth and train their salespeople to become great negotiators and master dealmakers.

This book is also a result of a disappointment. I have seen many training companies charging outrageously high prices to businesses in China or elsewhere in order to train their sales team on how to sell and negotiate. Unfortunately, many of those trainings confuse sales processes and sales attitude. Instead of sending a facilitator or a trainer to the company, they send a motivational speaker. Even the training's headlines look suspicious. It reads something like this: "Increase your sales by 35% in less than 1 month 'or' 88% of sales representatives experienced stellar growth in their sales after this training". I have nothing against motivational speakers, but I believe what companies need the most today is to help their people acquire skills and tools to compete in the marketplace.This book is priced at a low price so we can get it in the hands of every salesperson in China. I hope it will serve Chinese businesses and help them succeed in domestic and international market.

Abdelhak Benkerroum

Eastheimer International

序言 2

销售是一项情绪体验。从本质上来讲，销售是一个人把自己的信念转移给另一个人的行为。本书将会详细讨论销售的流程，让你在推销自己的产品、服务、想法的时候能有一种愉悦的体验。你将会学到如何识别他人的隐形需求，如何表述他们的执念和担忧，如何影响他人的决定，以及如何与他人建立信任。

本书第一版是在一年前出版的，成百上千的读者已经读过并在自己的日常工作和生活中践行了本书的理念。我在写这本书的时候，曾经设想过有共鸣的理想读者，他们应该是立足于中国，但跟海外客户有非常多的生意往来的销售人员以及他们的经理们。让我惊讶的是，这本书的大部分读者竟然来自各行各业，有一些人甚至从未接触过销售领域。通过跟这些读者的交流，我认识到：

- 我的很多商学院的学生喜欢研究理论，但很多职业经理人不喜欢。职业经理人想要实用的工具以便快速地解决业务中遇到的实际问题。这本书可以让他们如愿。
- 现在，中国的商业正在以前所未有的速度发展，每个人都很忙。花一个月的时间读一本小说可以让人接受，但花同样的时间读一本实用的销售技能书就不能让人接受了。我不是一个喜欢长篇大论的人，没办法把一个想法用 50 页的内容表述出来。在本书中，每一页你都能发现至少一个值得你思考的新观点。

Preface2

Selling is an emotional human experiment. It is, at its core, the act of transferring a powerful conviction from one person to another. This happens through an exchange that follows a process we will be discussing in details in this book in order to help you have a pleasant experiment when selling your products, your services, or your ideas. You will learn how to identify the hidden needs of the other party, how to address their resistances and fears, how to influence their decisions, and how to build trust with them.

Since the publication of the first edition of this book one year ago, thousands of people have had the opportunity to read it and apply its concepts in their daily lives. When I wrote *We Have a Deal,* I had in mind a specific audience that I wanted my messages to resonate with. That ideal audience was Chinese salespeople and their managers, operating in China but having extensive dealings with foreign counterparts. I was surprised later on to find out that a large audience that read this book is made up of people from all walks of lives, with some who have never been involved directly in sales nor have an immediate interest in doing so. When exchanging with these audiences, I came to the realization that:

- While a lot of my students at business schools enjoy diving into theories, most professional people don't. They want practical tools and quick fixes they can go ahead and implement in their business today. This book gives them that.
- Today Chinese businesses move faster than ever and everyone is in a hurry. It's OK to spend one month reading a novel, but it's not OK to spend that much time reading a practical sales book. I'm not a big fan of taking one single

- 基于销售的复杂性和不确定性，人们在销售的过程中会遇到各种不同的问题和担忧。有一个问题基本上每个人都会遇到——如何让我们的业务量增长，并可持续地发展下去？本书会在这个方面给你一些帮助。如果你是一个单打独斗的“格斗型”销售，那么这将是一个非常好的机会去成长为一名“全能型”销售。
- 无论与哪个国家的客户开展合作，销售人员都是关系的建立者。他们需要通过语言和行为与对方建立信任。在本书的第一版里，我没有进一步介绍这一内容，在这一版中我将对其进行深入分析。
- 有一个问题困扰着几乎所有的销售人员，无论他们多么优秀，那就是“借口管理”。潜在买家总是用各种借口和幌子不和你成交。在本书中，我会在这个方面给大家分享更多，希望能帮助读者们开启一扇门，找到处理买家借口的最佳方法。

基于这些认识，我赞同出版社发行第二版的建议。我非常感谢出版社对我的一如既往的支持。同时也很感谢每一个协助传播该书的部门，包括青岛市跨境电子商务协会，江苏、浙江、上海的工厂和贸易公司，以及中国各地的读书俱乐部。我不再罗列其他对本书做出贡献的人，因为我怕会漏掉一些人。但是每一位全程支持我的人，我知道你们是谁。我在此对你们表示诚挚的谢意和感激。

在大家开始阅读《优势成交：老外这样做销售（第二版）》这本书之前，有一件事希望大家能记在脑海中。每一个销售员都是 3 个身份的集合：市场人员、销售人员和客服人员。市场人员把马牵到水边，销售人员让马喝水，客服人员让马留在原地喝更多的水。如果市场人员没有给出有吸引力的信息，马就无法被牵到水边；如果销售人员没有把水的真正价值适当地

idea and massaging it across 50 pages. In almost every page of this book, you will come across at least one new idea that is worth pondering over.

- People in business have different questions and worries depending on multiple variables. But one question remains the same across the board: How can we grow our business and make it sustainable? This book will help you in that aspect. If you were an uncoordinated "street fighter" type of salesperson, here is your chance to become a fine "martial art master."
- Salespeople are relationship builders, no matter in which country's customer they operate. They need to establish trust with the other party through words and through actions. In the first edition of this book, I have not talked extensively about this part of the life of a salesperson. In this edition, I do.
- There is a specific area where salespeople still struggle with, no matter how good they are. And that is the "Objection handling" part. Potential buyers come up with all types of excuses and resistances to not buy from you. In this edition, I have elaborated a bit more on this area and hope that will help readers initiate a discussion internally regarding the best ways to handle buyer's resistances.

Going from those realizations, I agreed with the publisher of this book to release a 2nd edition. I want to thank them for their continuous support. I also want to thank everyone who helped promote and spread this book, from Qingdao e-commerce association, to factories and trading companies in Jiangsu, Zhejiang, Shanghai, and to book reading clubs all across China. I hesitate to mention names of people who have contributed in making this book a great one, because I always end up forgetting someone. But to those who have been there for me throughout the process, I know who you are. To you I am grateful.

Before I let you dive into *We Have a Deal*, there is a beautiful image I want every reader to keep in mind while reading this book. Every business is a

表达出来，马也不会喝水；如果客服人员不能让马喜欢上喝水的过程，他们也不能让马停留更长时间且喝更多的水。马指的就是客户，水就是你的产品。

阿道

宁波东方海默信息咨询有限公司

中国，上海

combination of three things: Marketing, Sales, and Customer Service. Marketing people bring the horse to the water, Salespeople make the horse drink, Customer Service people make the horse stay there and drink more. Marketing people can't bring the horse to the water if they don't design an attractive message that resonates with him. Salespeople can't make the horse drink if they don't properly demonstrate the true value of their water. Customer Service people can't make the horse stay and drink more if they don't make him enjoy that experience. The horse is the customer, and the water is your product.

AbdelhakBenkerroum
Eastheimer International
Shanghai, China

目　录

第一部分　从辨识客户到最终成交

第二部分　打造一支优秀的销售团队

CONTENTS

Part 1 From Probing the Prospect to Closing the Deal

Part 2 Building an Outstanding Sales Team

第三部分　老外眼中的中国销售

Part 3 Chinese Salespeople Through a Foreigner's Eyes

| 第一部分 |

从辨识客户到最终成交

销售流程不可一概而论，汽车、玩具、珠宝等行业的销售流程各不相同。但不论销售所处的情境如何，其背后的逻辑大体上是相同的，比如制定销售策略、辨识并搞定潜在客户。本部分旨在讲解这些共通的流程。这一部分将带你领略销售流程的各个阶段，并为你提供一些经过转化能够用于你所在公司具体情境的商业实例。这样的调整是很有必要的，特别是当你的公司同时运用两种不同的销售策略时：一是线上销售，一是线下销售。

本部分的后半部分主要讲的是销售过程中的“阻力应对”。这是因为每位潜在客户都有抵触你的产品、购买你竞争对手产品的理由和借口。潜在客户只有在极少数的情况下不会去质疑你的产品价格或产品质量。因此，你用于回应这些情况的方式也将决定你是否能够成功地完成一笔交易。

| Part 1 |

From Probing the Prospect to Closing the Deal

The sales process differs depending on whether your company is selling cars, toys or gold jewelry, but the logic is pretty much the same no matter where the sale takes place. It is a matter of setting a sales strategy, identifying the right prospect to engage with, then engaging with those prospects following a step-by-step process. This section is about that process. It will take you through the different phases of the sales process and provide you with a few examples that could be reframed and adjusted to fit your company's specific context. That adjustment would be relevant specifically if your company has two different sales strategies in place: one for online sales, and the other for offline sales.

A subsequent part of this section deals with the "objections handling" part of the process. The reason is that every prospect will have excuses and resistances to not buy from you and buy from the competition instead. There are very few cases where the potential buyers will not question your price, or the quality of your products, and so the way you respond to those situations/objections could determine whether you will be able to close that deal or not.

为谈判做好准备

孙子曾说：孰胜孰负，未战先知。意思是准备更充分的一方往往会获得战争的胜利，比如它拥有充足的供给、良好的训练、准确的情报、对地理地形的熟悉和掌控、精密的计划以及对敌情的全面掌握等。这是一项艰苦的工作，而且没有捷径，销售谈判也是如此。把销售谈判等同于战争是一种误导，不过两者确有相似之处，比如没有人能够准确预测结果，因为没有人知道事情到底会怎样发展。所以，你能做的就是通过制订行动计划来为各种偶发状况提前做准备。

一次常规且简明的销售谈判一般由谈判前准备，谈判中与潜在客户座谈、辨析客户需求、报价、消除潜在购买阻力、成交以及谈判后的后续跟进这几个环节组成，但有些环节可能不按顺序出现。比如你第一次出现在某潜在客户办公室的那一刻就有可能遇到购买阻力（被拒），一句简单的“你最近怎么样？我听说你的工厂近来面临一些生产上的难题”就有可能让你们的对话陷入僵局。在后面的章节我们会学习如何应对类似的阻力因素，现在先让我们来探讨下能够帮助你正确备战谈判，并以此提升成交率的六个建议。需要牢记的是，谈判相较于下棋，更像是一种扑克游戏。即便拿着一手好牌你还是有可能会输，但如果你为各种可能性做好设想和计划，结果可能会好一些。这些计划你需要以书面形式记录下来，并在与客户谈判前与公司的管理层交流分享。我过去常以喝下午茶的方式与我的团队一起准备重要的谈判。这种做法大错特错！除非聊天内容被记录下来，否则我和我的团队将带着不同的结论去参加谈判，这会有意见不一致的风险。

显然，这些记录便是“作战计划”，我们并不希望它落入客户的手中。

Preparing for a negotiation

Sun Tzu said that "Every battle is won or lost before it is ever fought". The battle would likely go to whoever had prepared best; a combination of the best supplies, the best training, the best intelligence, the best control of the ground, the best planning, the best understanding of the enemy, etc. It's hard work and there are no shortcuts. The same could be said about a sales negotiation. It might be misguided to equate a sales negotiation to a war, but they share a similarity in that no one can predict the outcome accurately because no one knows exactly how things will develop. However, what one can do is prepare for any contingencies by setting an action plan.

A normal and simplified form of a sales negotiation would consist of preparing for the meeting, sitting-down with the prospect, identifying his needs, making an offer, handling potential objections, closing the deal, and following-up, in that order. However, you might show up at a prospect's office and his first opening would be an objection. A simple "How have you been lately? I heard about the production challenges your factory has been facing" could take your discussion into a whole different direction. We will learn later how to handle similar objections, but let's first discuss the 6 pointers that will help you prepare for a negotiation properly so you improve your odds of closing the deal. One need to bear in mind that negotiation is more of a poker game than a chess game. You can still lose despite optimal preparation, but you would be better off planning for potential scenarios that might play out. That planning phase needs to be documented in written, and shared with the company's management before engaging prospects.I used to prepare for my important negotiations by sitting with my team around an afternoon tea and chatting. Big mistake! Unless this information is documented, I end up going to a meeting where my team and I "don't speak with the same voice", hence risking to sound uncoordinated.

Obviously, since that document is our "game plan",we don't want the customer to get his hands on it.

提示1：我应该谈判吗？

可协商性并非意味着所有事都必须谈判。有时花费在谈判上的时间与产出根本不成正比。比如一位想买全新大屏电视的英语教师在网上做了大量有关电视型号和费用的调查，逛了好几个电子产品商店，确定了电视及安装的整体价格以及自己要订阅的频道。之后他又去逛电子产品商店，最终获得了100美元的优惠。这样的案例能被视作一次成功的谈判吗？恐怕不行。事实是，这名教师回到家告诉妻子："我购物省了100美元！"他的妻子问他："你在这笔交易上总共花了多少时间？"教师说："20个小时。"妻子厉声说："所以你的时间只值每小时5美元吗？"

在决定是否要谈判时，你应该考虑你是否想谈判以及谈判的潜在风险和回报有哪些。因为买家或卖家在一次谈判上所花费的时间也可以用在其他重要的事情上，这被称为"机会成本"。有时那些低回报率的谈判并不值得你花费那么多的时间。

提示2：我们是谁以及我们要做些什么？是什么让我们与众不同？

每个销售代表都应该以非常简洁的方式（在15~20秒内）介绍自己以及公司的业务情况。排练一两句话，并时刻准备着在展会、联谊会甚至是一次简单的介绍中派上用场，这被称为"电梯法则"——在共同乘电梯的几十秒内将重要信息传达给潜在客户，同时引起对方的兴趣与注意。在琢磨你的话术时，想想你将和谁同乘一部电梯，并根据不同的目标对象在话术上做一些细微的调整。如果你正在准备一次销售谈判，那你已经知道你的潜在客户是

Pointer 1: Should I negotiate?

Just because everything is negotiable doesn't mean that everything has to be negotiated. Sometimes the time spent on negotiating is not worth the investment. Take the case of an English teacher who wants to buy a new big-screen TV. He does a lot of research online on TV's models and costs, then visits several electronic shops. He then settles for a combined price package of TV with installation along with a subscription for his preferred channels. He goes back to visit a few electronic shops, and manages to obtain a price concession of 100 USD. Could that be considered a successful negotiation? Not necessarily. Here is what happened: The teacher arrived home and told his wife: "I saved 100 USD on my purchase!" His wife replied: "How much time in total did you spend on this transaction?" The professor answered: "20 hours in total". His wife snapped: "Is your time worth 5 USD per hour?"

Before making a decision about whether to negotiate or not, you should consider your feeling about negotiating, and the potential risks and rewards. The time a buyer or seller spends on a negotiation is a time that could be spent on other vital tasks. These are called "opportunity cost". Sometimes it is just not worth it to spend that time on other less rewarding tasks such as a low-value added negotiation.

Pointer 2: Who are we and what do we do?And what makes us special?

Every sales representative should be able to articulate in a very simple way（in 15–20 seconds）who they are and what they do as a company. A sentence or two should be learned, rehearsed, and ready with you to be recited in a fair, at a networking event, or as a simple introduction. It is called an "Elevator Pitch", because you should be able to deliver it in a time span of an elevator ride and still be able to spark interest and generate excitement. When crafting your pitch, think about who you will be with in the elevator,

谁了。我曾任职的一家美国物流公司在运用“电梯法则”时，用一个通用的话术来介绍“我们是谁以及我们要做些什么”：

“我们是一家帮助客户加强物流网络及供应链运作的美国500强跨国公司。我们的业务涉及海、陆、空运输以及海关清关、订单管理、仓储服务等。”

如果你的产品或服务是为了满足客户多方面的需求，优先介绍对客户最重要的那些。我在展会上运用“电梯法则”时，总会加上一句：“那您呢？”这样一来对话就不会中断。

“什么让你与众不同”的意思是你们公司与竞争对手相比有哪些优势。那些让你们公司显得更有价值的特性是什么。例如你去参加一个面试，面试官已经见过几个候选人了。有一些候选人跟你来自同一所学校，他们是你的竞争对手，跟你一样想要得到那个职位。你会跟面试官说些什么让自己脱颖而出，吸引他的注意力，给他留下深刻的印象？什么让你与众不同？现在，将这个逻辑用在你的销售工作上。

提示3：我的潜在客户是谁以及他的需求或问题是什么？

每个产品或服务都旨在满足一种需求，或解决一个问题，或两者兼备，请记好这句话。让我再重复一遍：每个产品或服务都旨在满足一种需求，或解决一个问题，或两者兼备。有的公司可以创造需求，比如第一个发明触屏手机的公司。当时，没有人知道自己需要触屏手机，直到这种产品被推入市场。作为一名销售人员，你的职责便是辨识客户（或潜在客户）的需求，或者你可以为他们解决的难题。如果你的潜在客户是一家上市公司，这项工作会容易得多，因为他们的数据和记录都提交给了政府有关部门并向社会公众公开。如果客户不是上市公司，那就只能靠自己利用各种资源来了解该公司

and slightly modify it depending on the target. If you are preparing for a sales meeting, then you already know who that prospect is. A US logistics company I worked for in the past had a straight forward "Elevator Pitch" that described "who we are and what we did". It went something like this:

"We are a US Fortune 500 multinationals that helps customers drive performance improvements in their logistics networks and supply-chain practices. Our services range from sea, land and air transportation to customs clearance, order management and warehousing."

If your product or service serves several needs, prioritize and stick with the most important ones. When I recite my pitch at a fair, I almost always follow up with "How about you?" so the conversation keeps flowing.

What makes you special is something at which your company is better than the competitors. Something that positions your company's value as higher than others'. Think of it as if you are going for a job interview, and the hiring manager has already met several candidates that day. Some of those candidates went to the same school as you. Those candidates are your competitors, competing for that same position you want to obtain. What would you tell the hiring manager to stand out, to impress him, to leave an excellent impression? What makes you different from everyone else? Now apply the same logic to your business.

Pointer 3: Who is my prospect and what are his needs or problems?

Every product or service aims at either fulfilling a need, or solving a problem, or both. Remember this statement well. Let me repeat it: Every product or service aims at either fulfilling a need, or solving a problem, or both. Some companies create that need, like the first company that invented the touchscreen phone. No one knew they needed one until it was created and marketed properly. Your job as a salesman is to understand what are the customer's (or prospect's) needs, or what challenges he is facing that you can solve. If it is a publicly traded company, then that task is made easier since

的情况了。资源可以是该公司的前职员、服务提供者或是客户等。

客户的竞争对手常常是我最佳的情报来源。如果我跟潜在客户或者当前客户聊，我一定会问他们几个关于竞争对手的问题。他们会毫不犹豫地与我分享对方的问题和困境。基于这些信息，我可以拿我的产品和服务去联系他们。我会找到客户的那些竞争对手，跟他们说："我听闻你们正面临这样、那样的挑战，我想跟您讨论下我们如何帮您克服这些困难。"

如今的公司都非常乐意分享自己的日常活动。快速浏览一家公司的博客或者社交媒体账号就可以获得远超你想象的诸多资讯。这类资讯在其雇员的个人社交媒体账号上展现得更为直白。在这些社交平台上你可以看到潜在客户的员工在庆典期间与竞争者的员工的合影；该公司在另一个城市举办的一次活动；其在工厂里发生的一次事件；公司员工一次针对他国客户的拜访等。销售人员在与潜在客户谈判前必须有所准备，你要知道他们是谁、他们是做什么的，以及他们的需求是什么。

还有一个不常用到的方法：每周都到你所在城市的港口去查看集装箱的进出、货物的装卸、进口货物的检验报告、竞争者的卡车等。仅从潜在客户或竞争者暴露在外的供应链你就能获得大量的信息。

提示 4：我的弱点是什么？

在生意场上了解自己的弱点至关重要，你们公司的弱点也许就是竞争对手的优点。

每个公司都有其弱项或盲点，你的也不例外。如果你没有认清这个现实，那么你的问题就大了。在准备销售谈判时把你公司的主要弱项列出来至关重要。因为你的潜在客户很可能在谈判中提到这些，你要提前准备好答案以反驳

their data and records are made public on their quarterly filings with the government. If it is not, then it's up to you to have sources within the company that could help you know more about them.The sources could be a former employee, one of their service providers, one of their customers...

My best source of intelligence is often the customer's competitor. If I talk to a prospect or a client, I make sure I ask them a few questions about their competitors. They don't hesitate to share the competitor's problems and struggles. I can then take that information, and use it to target that competitor with my products and services. I would contact that competitor saying "I heard from the marketplace that you are facing challenges in this and that area of your business. I would like to meet with you and discuss how we can help you fix that."

Companies today are very generous when it comes to sharing what's going on in their daily lives. A quick look at a company's blog or social media account gives you more information than you could ask for. That information is shared even more candidly on the employees' personal social media accounts. Pictures with the competitor during a ceremony, an event organized in another city, an incident that happened in the factory, a trip to a foreign country to visit a customer, and so forth and so on. You have no excuses to show up at the prospect's facility without having minimum knowledge regarding who they are, what they do, and what are their needs.

Another way that is not often explored is to make it a rule to go to the port of your city on a weekly basis to check out the containers arriving or leaving, the commodities offloaded, the inspection reports, the competitors' trucks…There is so much information that can be gathered about the prospect or the competitor just by looking at the part of their supply-chain that is left exposed to the general public.

Pointer 4: What are my weaknesses?

It is important to know your weaknesses as a business because your company's weaknesses might be your competitor's advantages. Every business has its

对方。理想状态下，你准备的回答应该解释你的公司打算如何解决或处理这些弱项。例如："我们意识到我们的客户服务在过去的几周里有些滞后。这是因为我们对公司内部做的一些调整影响到了这方面的表现。我们将两名客服代表调职到了市场部，这次调动增加了其他客服代表的工作负担。我们已经招聘了三名新职员，并且正对他们进行培训。现在我们客服部门的服务能力有了显著提高。"意识到自己的弱项是好事，除此之外知道如何去解决它们，以及如何以正确的方式对涉及它们的问题进行沟通也是一项宝贵的技能。我们最不希望客户担心的就是："这家公司连自己的问题都解决不了，我怎么相信它能解决我的问题？"

你可能会疑惑，世界另一端的这些外国客户是如何知道你的弱点的呢？你的竞争对手会告诉他们。

提示 5：如何衡量我的金钱与非金钱让步？

谈判无非就是给予和索取的较量。你不能指望在谈判中，一拿到自己想要的，就扭头走人。请记住：你应该提前列出一份你能够与谈判对手进行交易的金钱以及非金钱条目清单，以此推进谈判的进度。请注意我用的词是"交易"而非"赠送"，因为让步本身就是给予和索取过程中的一部分。

该清单不仅需要包含那些很难做出让步的条目，也要包含那些轻易就可以妥协的条目。不管你如何来排列它们，你都应该在谈判期间表现出你做出的每个让步都是你本次交易的一个痛点。你一定不想在没得到任何回报之前就轻易地向谈判对手摊牌。

关于金钱（价格）让步，你要确保事先知道"盈亏平衡点"，即本次交易成交价如果低于某个价格的话，你的生意就没有利润可言。所以你得为谈判做充分准备以示你要成交的决心。

weaknesses or blind spots. Yours certainly does too. If you do not recognize that fact, then your problem is bigger. It is important to list your main company's weaknesses during the preparation for the sales negotiation, along with potential responses to reply back to the prospect in case they invoke them during the talks. Ideally, the responses you prepare should explain how your company intends to fix or address those weaknesses. For example, "we are aware that our customer service was lagging behind the last few weeks. This is due to the fact that we had a few changes internally that affected our performance. We have moved two of our customer service representatives to the Marketing department, and this move had increased the workload on the other customer service representatives. We have already hired three new people and they are undergoing a training currently. Our customer service department is fully functional right now." Being aware of one's weaknesses is a good thing. But knowing how to fix them and how to communicate properly about them is a valuable skill. The last thing we want our customers to think is: "This company is not able to solve its own problems. How can I trust them to solve mine?"

You are probably wondering "How could this foreign client sitting at the other side of the world hear about my weaknesses?" Don't worry. Your competitor is telling him about them.

Pointer 5: How do my monetary and non-monetary concessions rank?

Negotiation is about giving and taking. One can not plan to enter a negotiation, take what he wants, and walk away. Having that in mind, you should prepare a list of monetary and non-monetary items you can trade in order to move a discussion forward. Notice the use of the word "trade", not "give away" because concessions are part of a give-and-take process.

That list needs to have items ranked from the most difficult to let go, to the easiest to let go. Regardless of how you rank them, you should act during the meeting as if every concession is a painful one for your business. You don't want to

活动空间应该控制在一个特定的范围内。我看到很多公司告诉他们的销售人员产品的最低价，但是极少限定最高价。销售经理必须告诉业务员，“这是你可以向这个产品收取的最低价，这是你可以向客户索要的最高价。超出最高价，客户会感到被欺骗而抛弃你”。记住，很多潜在客户不会告诉你你的价格太高，他们会直接走开。

提示6：我的团队代表以及后备人员是谁?

我看到许多销售代表带着四五个人的团队走进客户的办公室，而在与客户交谈时并无他们的用武之地。在决定带谁和你一起去与潜在客户谈判时，问问自己与会人员的附加值是什么。如果他们只是坐着旁听，那还是让他们在办公室各司其职比较好。如果你销售的是科技产品，需要你的工程师在与会时解答技术方面的提问，这种情况下带上他／她参加会议也无妨。除非该客户通知我说他们希望一名细分产品经理或某个部门经理一同参与，否则我都喜欢独自参加销售谈判。在出发前，我会通知公司内部两三名可能会用到的核心人员，让他们做好准备，我随时可能通过电话与他们联系。如此一来，如果该客户在销售谈判期间问了一个我不知道的细节问题，我就可以直接连线相应人员，打开扬声器并寻求验证。这是在我曾经工作过的一家迪拜的供应链公司里学到的方法。我在一次销售谈判时被客户问到我们公司某个位于自贸区特定位置的仓库有多少可用空间，以及租一年的条件是什么。我当时并不知道具体的细节信息，就告诉他们我会在回到办公室后的第一时间予以答复。就在我回到办公室，从仓库经理那儿搜集信息再打电话给该名客户的那段时间，我丢了那桩生意。那名客户说他们已经找到了一家服务商，不再需要我们了。我后来了解到，那名客户在当天下午密集安排了与三家不同服

throw all your cards on the table easily without getting anything back in return.

Regarding the monetary concessions (price), I make sure I always know the "break even point" in advance. That's the price under which the transaction will not be profitable for my business. Then I get prepared to give enough movement during the negotiation to demonstrate that I want the business.

That movement should stay within a specific range. I saw companies telling their salespeople the lowest price they can quote to sell the product. But very few businesses go as far as setting the maximum price. It is important for the sales manager to tell his salespeople "This is the minimum price you can charge for this product. And this is the maximum price you charge a customer. Beyond that maximum pricing point, the customer might feel cheated and walk away." Remember many prospects won't tell you that your price is too high. They would just walk away if they feel that's the case.

Pointer 6: What' s my team representation and stand-by staff?

I have seen many sales representatives going into the customer's office in teams of 4 or 5 people, taking with them staff whose presence is not of need. On deciding who to take with you to a sales meeting with a prospect, ask yourself what value-added would that person bring to the table. If they will go to sit-down and listen, they would be better off staying at their desk doing their actual job. If, however, you have to make a technical sale, and you need the input of your engineer to answer technical questions on the spot, then there is no harm in taking him or her with you. I generally prefer to go alone to a sales meeting, unless the prospect informs me that they would like the input from a specific product manager or a division manager. Before leaving my office for an important sales meeting, I would inform 2 or 3 key people within my company whose input might be needed, and ask them to be ready to answer their cell phone in case I call them. That way, during the sales negotiation, when the customer asks a specific question for which I don't

务商的三场连续谈判。我们是第一场，而且我确信其余两家服务商早已事先准备好这两个问题的答案了，因此该客户才可以快速作出抉择。要是我在那时通过电话得到我们仓库经理的答复的话，或许那次销售谈判的结局就会大不相同。

我想补充一句，在很多文化中，把人按照年龄、性别、资历来划分是很常见的事情。换句话说，如果客户的决策人是位男士，那么就派一位男士销售人员去见他。如果客户年纪不小了，就派一位年龄大的销售人员接待他。在一些国家，经验是跟年龄捆绑在一起的，销售人员年纪越大，就会被认为越有经验。

作为局外人，我补充一点，我认为潜在客户同时与一家或好几家竞争者谈判，是一个好的信号。这意味着那名潜在客户是真的想要购买，除此之外他甚至还为该交易或项目设立了预算。所以成功与否完全取决于销售人员是否比其他竞争者更好地准备以及主导销售谈判。

“这是我们‘变换视角’倡议的一部分。”

have an answer, I could just pick-up the phone, call the concerned person, put her on speaker, and ask for clarifications. I learned that lesson when I used to work for a supply chain company in Dubai. I had a sales meeting where the customer asked for how much space we had available at one of our warehouses in a specific location at the Free Zone, and what terms apply for a yearly lease. I didn't have the exact details right there and then I said I would get them as soon as I got to my office. Just the time for me to go back to the office, gather the information from our warehouse manager, and call the prospect to give him the details he needed, the deal was gone. The customer said that they had already found a service provider and my input was not needed anymore. I learned afterward that the prospect had lined up three back-to-back meetings that afternoon with three different service providers. I was the first in-line, and I am sure the second and the third service providers had their answers ready, which allowed the prospect to make a quick decision. Had I called our warehouse manager on the spot to get an answer, maybe the outcome of the sales meeting would have been different.

在准备阶段花费时间的长短取决于这场销售谈判的复杂程度。一旦全部或大多数的要素都已经就绪，建议你通过一场模拟销售来练习如何在谈判中正确地使用它们。

销售团队常用的一项训练是让一位销售代表扮演卖家，另一位充当潜在买家，这个方法称为“角色转换”。它有助于你理解潜在客户的观点和视角，从而让你在面对他们的时候表现得更好。它还能帮你减轻压力，同时它也是一种办公室的趣味活动。许多美国政客在备战政治辩论时也多次使用过类似的训练。候选人扮演他自己，再由一位工作人员扮演其竞争对手。

I would add that it is common practice in some cultures to align people by age, gender, or seniority. In other words, if the decision maker from the customer's side is a male, then it's a male salesperson that goes to meet with him. If it's an old customer then it's an old salesperson that aligns with him. In some societies, experience is associated with age; the older a salesperson is, the likely it is for him to be perceived as experienced.

On the sideline of that, I would add that when a prospect has been talking to one or more competitors, I interpret it as a good sign. It means that the prospect is serious about buying and probably even have a budget set aside for that specific transaction or project. It's up to the salesperson to better prepare than the competition and lead a sales negotiation better than they do.

The amount of time spent on the preparation phase depends on how complex the sales negotiation might be. But once all or most of these elements are ready, it is recommended to go through a sales simulation to prepare how they can be used as the negotiation flows.

A common practice among sales teams is to ask one of the sales representatives to play the role of the seller, and another one to play the role of the potential buyer. This technique is called "Role Reversal". It pushes you to understand the prospect's perspectives and arguments, hence preparing you to better face them. It also helps alleviating the stress, and it's a fun activity to have at the office. A similar practice has been used in many instances by US politicians when preparing for a political debate. The candidate plays his own role and a staff member plays the role of the opponent.

识别你的潜在客户

在准备阶段还有一点需要考虑，我会用下面这个完整的章节来进行介绍，以示其重要性。如果你不断地听到你的潜在客户说“抱歉，我们对你的产品不感兴趣”，你或许应该停下来思考一下自己的销售对象是否正确。通过问自己“谁是我的客户”这样一个简单的问题，你就能得到答案。销售团队以及市场营销团队需要合作并展开头脑风暴，通过回答诸如“谁是我们的客户？我们应该争取什么样的潜在客户？谁准备购买我们的产品？我们可以根据规模、行业或者其他的相关变量来辨识目标客户吗？”等问题来延伸讨论。

这类讨论无疑揭示了这样一个普遍的事实：并非团队中的每个人都确切地知道他们的潜在客户是什么样的。另一个事实是：至少有一个参会的人认为“谁都可以成为我的客户”。

没有公司可以通过满足所有人的需求来获得成功。这一点对于处在“找自己”初期阶段的小公司尤其重要。你或许拥有业内最出色、最聪明的销售人员，但是如果你让他们向错误的潜在客户推销产品，那么他们不仅浪费了自己的时间，也浪费了你的金钱。销售经理有责任辨识潜在客户，并确定哪些信息能打动目标客户。毫无疑问，每家公司都有市场部门，其职责是甄选出真正的市场和正确的目标客户。

有些人认为确立更少的潜在客户，将会缩小企业的市场空间并使销售范围受限。恰恰相反，当我们知道自己想要销售的对象是谁时，我们才会知道如何分配资源。否则，我们将会不断地吃闭门羹，这就像我之前提到过的那样：你不仅会浪费时间、金钱，还会错失机遇。

Identifying the right customer

There is one more piece that goes into the preparation puzzle, but it deserves a full chapter on its own given its importance. If you keep hearing from your prospects "Sorry, but we are not interested in your product", then you might need to pause for a moment and figure out if you are trying to sell to the right prospects. This could be answered by asking yourself the simple question"Who should be my customer?" The sales team and marketing team need to get together and brainstorm over this topic by expanding the discussion to answer questions such as "Who is our customer? What prospects should we go after? Who is ready to buy our product? Can we define our target customer in terms of size, industry or any other relevant variable?"

That kind of discussion will undoubtedly reveal a common fact: Not everyone within the team knows exactly who their potential customer should look like. Another fact that will be revealed is that there is at least one person around the table who believes that "everyone could be my customer."

No company can succeed by being everything to everyone. This is particularly relevant for early stage small businesses that are trying to "find themselves". You can have the best and smartest salespeople in the industry, but if you are sending them to sell to the wrong prospects then they are wasting their time and your money. It falls under the responsibility of the sales manager to go through that process of clearly identifying who should be the ideal prospect, and how to target them with messages that resonate with that exact target audience.Needless to say that for companies that have a marketing department, the task of identifying the right market and the right target customers falls under the responsibility of the marketing department.

Some believe that by targeting fewer potential customers, they are narrowing the playing field and will limit their reach. It's the other way around. When we know who we want to sell to, we will know how to allocate our resources. When we

一般来讲，你的客户是那些可能购买你的产品、服务和 / 或使你获得收益的人或实体。无论这个道理听起来多么浅显易懂，在某些情况下还是很难作出判断。医药公司应该给谁分派他们的销售人员？给病人？不，应该给医生。虽然买家和最终的用户都是病人，但医生才是开医药处方的人。玩具公司应该把玩具卖给谁？是卖给想要玩具的孩子，还是负责买单的人？

亚马逊公司成功界定了客户群体，下面我们一起看一下这个优秀案例。亚马逊的使命宣言写道："我们的使命是成为全球最以客户为中心的公司，让客户能够寻找并发现他们可能需要在线购买的任何商品，致力于为客户提供尽可能最低的价格。"

尽管亚马逊有四类不同的客户，但他们毫不犹豫地宣称消费者是他们的主要客户。这意味着他们会将人力物力着重用于消费者这一客户群体。亚马逊是通过分析产品收益与潜在客户需求之间的关系，得出客户是谁以及如何排列其优先级的结论的。

对"谁是我的客户"这个问题进行头脑风暴通常能够帮助一支销售或者市场团队找到目标。在该目标范围内，会出现少数**理想型潜在客户**。我有个能够帮助销售团队找到理想型潜在客户的快速训练，借助此项训练，销售人员在面对客户时就能够辨识出其是不是自己的目标客户。

把你目前最重要的 25 个客户列出来，然后想想是什么标准使他们如此理想。你将会用到两类标准：人口统计学和消费心理学。前者让你可以根据地区、规模、员工数量以及行业等类别划分客户群体，后者可以让你根据不可量化的变量来划分客户。以下便是一个消费心理学的应用实例：

- 已有的客户喜欢你的公司吗？
- 他们认可你的客户服务水平吗？

don't, we will keep knocking on doors, and being rejected, which goes back to the same issue mentioned above: You'll be wasting time, money, and opportunity.

Broadly speaking, your customers are people or entities who might be ready to buy your products, services and/or supply your revenue. However simple this statement might sound, there are a few cases where it gets difficult. To whom should drug companies send their salespeople? To the patients? No, to the doctors, because doctors are the ones who write the prescriptions even though the buyers and final users are the patients. And to whom should toy companies market their toys? To the kids who claim them? Or to the buyers who pay for them.

A good example is the way the company Amazon has successfully defined its customers. Amazon's mission statement says: "Our vision is to be Earth's most customer-centric company, to build a place where people can come to find and discover anything they might want to buy online, and endeavors to offer its customers the lowest possible price."

Though Amazon has four different customers, they don't hesitate to declare the Consumers as their primary customer. That means their resources go heavily and aggressively on developing the first type, which is "Consumers". What Amazon did is analyze the correlation between its product's benefits and the prospect's needs, then reach the conclusion regarding who their customers are, and how do they rank on their priorities list.

Brainstorming over the "Who is my customer" question will generally help a sales or marketing team find its target. Within that target, a few prospects will qualify as **ideal**. There is a quick exercise that can be performed to help the team find the ideal prospect so they learn how to recognize one when they see it.

Make a list of your top 25 current customers, and think of which criteria makes them ideal. There are two types of criteria that you will use: Demographics and Psychographics. The former allows you to split your customers by location, size, number of employees, industry... The latter allows you to split your customers relying on less quantifiable variables. An example of Psychographics that are used:

■ Do these existing customers love your company?

■ 他们准时付费吗？

■ 他们会与你定期会面吗？

■ 他们会和朋友、同事谈起你吗？

■ 他们会与你坦率交谈吗？

■ 他们会和你谈论如何改善你的商业现状吗？

从消费心理学的角度出发，用 1 到 10 级来评估每一名现有客户的每一条标准，10 级代表“理想”，1 级代表“完全不理想”。

一旦销售团队完成这个训练，他们就可以得到排名并评定哪些公司称得上是理想型客户。知道了理想型客户是什么样子之后，销售代表也就知道了谁才是他们预期的跟进对象。如果该排名上的前 25 家公司中的绝大部分最终被认定为非理想型客户，那么你的目标排名策略一定在某个地方出了问题。

出于策略考虑，一些公司会将市场部和销售部分开，还有一些公司则会将它们合为一体。无论在哪种情况下，市场团队参与辨识理想型潜在客户（消费者）都尤为重要。

理想型潜在客户一旦被确定下来，在谈及资源配置时就不得不考虑有关客户企业规模的问题。一家公司是不是应该先着眼于小企业客户，然后再转向大企业客户呢？

根据你公司规模和性质的不同，“小企业客户”有着不同的定义。一支组织良好的销售团队一定有一个文档齐全的客户数据库，以规模、地区、收益、发展潜力等因素分类。举个例子，通过收益来对现有的客户进行排名是个不错的资源分配指标：

■ A 客户：超过 10,000 美元；

■ B 客户：2,000 到 10,000 美元；

- Do they appreciate your customer service?
- Do they pay their invoices on time?
- Do they meet with you regularly?
- Do they tell their friends and colleagues about you?
- Do they speak with you honestly and candidly?
- Do they tell you what improvements you can bring to the current business?

For these Psychographics, a scale from 1 to 10 is used to evaluate each existing customer per criteria, where 10 being "ideal" and 1 being "not ideal at all".

Once the sales team has completed this task, they will be able to take a look at the ranking, and assess which companies qualify as being the most ideal customers. By knowing how an ideal customer looks like, sales representatives will know who they should go after in their prospection. If most of the companies on that top 25 list end up being not ideal, then there is a problem somewhere in the targeting strategy.

For strategic purposes, some companies segregate the marketing department and sales department. Some others have the two teams overlapping. In either case, it is important for the marketing team to take part in this process of identifying the ideal prospect or customer.

Once the ideal prospects are identified, a question of size will certainly come up when the discussion starts moving towards resources allocations. Is it relevant for a company to target small businesses first, then move on to large businesses later on?

"Small customers" can mean different things depending on the size and nature of your business. A well-organized sales team will always have a well documented customers' database that contains enough information identifying customers by size, geography, revenue contribution, potential for growth… For example, ranking existing customers by revenue contribution is a good indicator of how resources can be allocated:

- A account: More than 10,000 USD
- B account: 2,000 USD to 10,000 USD
- C account: Up to 2,000 USD

■ C 客户：最多 2,000 美元。

新年来临的时候，我便知道到邀请一些 A 类客户吃饭的时候了，尤其是当他们欠我钱的时候。如果我们要组织一场新产品或新服务的发布会，那么需要确保对 C 类和 B 类客户投入更大的精力，以便获得最佳反响。

我曾自己经营过一个小企业，有一份仅含大客户的“A 类客户”列表。大客户便意味着大机会，不过随之而来的挑战也更大。在负责管理自己的小公司时，我需要向股东汇报工作，或者给予风险投资者投资回报，如此巨大的压力迅速地榨干了我的资源。尽管大客户不尽相同，但在与美国财富 500 强企业打交道的经历中，我一次又一次地看到了这样的趋势。因此，如果你执意与大客户共事，就需要注意几个现实问题。

现实 1：繁重的合同扼杀了小企业

一家跨国公司给你的合同足有“半斤重”，这不仅会消耗你宝贵的时间，还会消耗你的金钱。你需要雇佣一名律师（价格高昂的那种）来检查合同，并且你需要花费无数时间拿着记号笔对合同进行标注。如果你正好乐于这么做的话，这将是一项有趣的工作。但就我个人而言，我对此并不感兴趣。在迪拜工作时，我曾经负责一位石油与天然气产业的客户，该客户单是在供应链和物流服务方面就为我们创造了每年数百万美元的收入。他们的合同被称为主服务协议，共有 200 多页，涵盖我们全球层面的交易信息，涉及六大洲的 50 个国家。不仅如此，每个国家还有一份有关具体运营和监管的本土服务协议，每份都有 20 多页。现在要是让我在花时间与昂贵的律师探讨重点标记文件和花时间改进自己的产品和服务之间选择的话，你猜我会怎么选？别误

When the new year rolls around, I know I will need to invite some A Customers to dinner especially if they owe me money. If we organize an event to launch a new product or service, we make sure more effort is directed towards C and B customers for optimum engagement.

I was a small-business owner myself and I had an "A customers" list made exclusively of large structures. Big companies can come with big opportunities, but they also come with big headaches. When I am in charge of driving the growth of my small company and I have shareholders to report to or venture capitalists to pay back, adding the pressure of a behemoth can dry my resources quickly. Of course all big companies are not the same, but in my experience dealing with US Fortune 500 companies, I saw tendencies that kept coming up again and again. So if you decide to go ahead and engage strongly with large customers anyways, you need to be aware of a few realities.

Reality 1: Heavy contracts kill small businesses

A multinational will present you with a "half kilogram" contract that will drain your valuable time and drain your valuable money. You will hire a lawyer (an expensive one) to go through it and you will spend countless hours with a highlighter in your hand. The exercise could be fun if that is what you enjoy doing. I am personally not a big fan of that. Back in Dubai, I managed an Oil and Gas customer with whom we made millions of dollars of revenue per year in supply chain and logistics services only. Their contract, called a Master Service Agreement, was over 200 pages long and was covering our transactions on a global level, in 50 countries of 6 continents. In addition to that, we had a Local Service Agreement that dealt with specific operational and regulatory requirements per country. And those were over 20 pages each. Now, if I had to choose between spending time on the phone talking to expensive lawyers with a highlighter in my hand versus spending time to drive product and service improvements, guess which one I would choose. Don't get me wrong, one could use that process as a learning opportunity.

会，你可以把这个过程视为一种学习的机会。通过这个过程，我对服务范围、价格机制、关键绩效指标、商业道德准则、报告要求等方面都有了更好的理解。但是我曾任职的这家公司是一家跨国企业，而非一家小公司。我从不同的副总裁以及产品经理那儿得到了极大的支持。想象一下你的小公司要全靠你自己处理这些繁杂的流程，那该是多么大的资源浪费啊！

现实 2：频繁的价格谈判并非趣事

无论你喜欢与否，大客户都会在价格以及条款上无情地压制你。原因就在于大客户通常在涉及价格与合同条款时拥有强大的谈判能力。许多公司内部都设有完善的采购部门，他们唯一的工作就是采购。衡量该部门表现的指标之一就是看他们每年同比为公司节省了多少资金。相信我，这些老行家在运用强势的采购技巧时会变得非常有创意。我之前在巴黎工作时，我们公司的一个国际客户正计划着发布一份全球需求建议书（RFP）来外包他们的供应链服务管理。我们公司和该客户在世界多地都有合作，但是他们还是决定推出这份 RFP，并从新的业务范围的不同供应链服务商那儿获得新的报价。在他们推出该 RFP 之前，他们还向所有现有的服务提供商发送了邮件，要求他们降低几个区域的现有价格以显示自己“承诺与我们合作并抛出橄榄枝”的意向。结果他们还没有推出该 RFP，供应链服务商就降价了！

我的一个国际客户在这一点上做得更加深入。他们曾告诉我：“这是我们需要的货物，这是我们要求的时间节点，这是我们认可的价格。如果你们同意这些条款，我们就合作这个项目，如果你们不同意，就以后再合作吧。”

Throughout the process, I gained good understanding of the scope of services, pricing mechanisms, KPI's, business ethics policies, reporting requirements…But I was working for a multinational, not a small company. I received strong support from various VP's and product managers. Imagine your small company going through this hideous process all on its own. What a waste!

Reality 2: Frequent rates negotiations are not fun

Whether you like it or not, a large customer will squeeze you mercilessly on prices and terms and conditions. The reason is that large customers happen to have substantial negotiation power when it comes to negotiating rates and terms. Many companies have a well established procurement department whose sole job is to buy and procure. One of the indicators of that department's performance is how much cash it is saving for the company year-over-year. And believe me, those old sharks get very creative when it comes to using aggressive buying techniques. Back when I worked in Paris, one of our global customers was planning to release a global Request For Proposal (RFP) to outsource the management of their supply chain services. We already had existing business with that customer in various locations around the world. But they decided to release the RFP to get new prices from various supply chain services providers based on the new scope of business. Before they even released the RFP, they mailed a letter to all their current service providers to ask them to reduce existing prices in several areas to show, as they put it, a "commitment to do business with our company and as a gesture of good intention". They did not release the RFP yet and they were already asking their supply chain services providers to decrease prices!

Another one of our global clients took it one step further. They used to tell us: Here is what we need, here is when we need it, and here is how much we will pay for it. If you agree to these terms let's work on this project. If you don't, then wait for the next opportunity.

现实3：你的企业真的准备好接纳大客户了吗?

你或许在向大型跨国企业销售产品或服务方面很成功，不过现在你需要回答一个简单的问题：你的公司有服务这个客户的资源吗？这些资源包括人力、物力以及财力。

- 人力资源指的是你需要配备具有专业技能且态度端正的人员与大客户接触。
- 物力资源由充足的原材料供应、足够的仓储空间或任何其他的有形资源组成。
- 财力资源意味着拥有充足的现金流以适应大客户在交易完成后的45天或60天付款。

如果你对上述问题的回答都是肯定的，那么就没有问题。只要确保你不是“二八法则”（80%的销售来自20%的客户）的受害者就可以。如果你陷入了“二八法则”困境，谈判力的平衡就会偏向并有利于客户，而这种情况并非是你希望在谈判过程中遇到的。

现实4：建立关系并非易事

建立关系是“建立信任”的西式说法。如果你是与跨国公司合作的一家小公司，你将需要花费大量的时间将该跨国公司的主管和你的团队成员统一起来，以此建立你们两家公司的相互依存关系。你会很快发现以下事实：

- 一家跨国公司的CEO并不会与经营小公司的你定期开会，除非他计划收购你的公司；

Reality 3: Are your operations really ready to accommodate large accounts?

You might be successful in selling your product or service to a large multinational, but here you will need to answer a simple question: Does your company have the resources to service this account properly? Those resources need to consist of human, material, and capital resources.

- Human resources means having the right people with the right skills and attitudes to engage with a large customer.
- Material resources could consist of having enough raw material supplies or enough warehouse space or any other tangible resources.
- Capital resources means having enough cash-flow to accommodate a large customer that will pay 45 or 60 days after the transaction is completed.

If the answer is yes to the above, (it's) good for you. Just make sure you are not victim of the Pareto Principle where "80% of your sales come from 20% of your clients." If you fall into that trap, the negotiation power balance will tilt to the customer's advantage and that's not a position you want to be in when you sit down at the negotiation table.

Reality 4: Building relationship is challenging

Building relationship is the western way of saying "building trust". If you're a small company dealing with a multinational, you'll need to spend much time on aligning executives and team members to create interdependencies between your two companies. You will soon find out the following realities:

- The CEO of a multinational will not necessarily be able to go on regular meetings with you, the little owner of a small business, unless he plans to buy you.

- 你将花费大量的时间来弄清楚客户公司内部谁做什么或者其某个特定部门是做什么的；
- 很难找到实际的决策者。你或许会认为那个采购经理有权做决定并能裁定是否交易，其实不一定是这样的，在一些公司里，采购经理的职责包括搜集供应商的报价和提议，审查这些报价和提议并提交给副总裁，最终由副总裁决定谁来负责这笔交易；
- 大公司部门之间有相对较长的周转期，有时是在不同国家的分公司之间进行。

曾有些在全球范围内为沃尔玛服务的小企业主告诉我：与著名的财富 500 强企业合作让他们获得了更多曝光率。我对他们的这个说法表示赞同。把沃尔玛作为客户是你和新的潜在客户交谈时的一个不错卖点。不过这要付出什么样的代价呢?

仅在一种情况下大客户的附加值才不枉你的小公司在合作的过程中所花费的精力，那就是你能在合作的过程中学到东西。毫无疑问，大客户会有严格的要求而且你获得的利润较低，但是他们能帮你有效地精简公司流程。你将从他们那儿学到如何更好地进行合同谈判、如何遵守监管要求、如何优化生产等。德国企业阿迪达斯的大部分产品从亚洲购进。它在中国寻找有创新能力的或者能提供大量高品质、低价格产品的潜力供应商。德国人讨厌退货，因此，阿迪达斯在德国总部建立了一支专家团队，专门考察新供应商的工厂并与他们的管理人员交流，帮助他们在生产和供应链方面提升效率以适应业务需要。

重要提醒：在分派你的销售团队前往该跨国公司前，你要知道你将面对什么挑战。

- You will spend countless hours trying to figure out who does what at the customer's side or sometimes within a specific department at the customer's side.
- Getting to the actual decision maker could be hard. You might be thinking that a sourcing manager is empowered to make decisions and award businesses. Not always. In some companies, the sourcing manager's role consists of gathering quotes and proposals from suppliers, reviewing them, and submitting them to the Vice President who will make a decision on who to award the business to.
- Large companies have relatively big turnover between departments, between divisions, or sometimes between branches in different countries.

I was told by some small business owners who service Walmart on a global level that having a well-known Fortune 500 company as their customer gives them exposure. I agree with them. Having Walmart as a customer is a good selling point when you talk to new prospects. But at what cost?

There is only one instance where the value added of a large customer could be justified by the hassle your small business will go through. And that is the learning process. The larger customer will undoubtedly have strict requirements and offer low margins, but the help they will provide in streamlining your company's own processes is extremely useful. You will learn from them how to better negotiate contracts, how to abide by regulatory requirements, how to optimize your production… and the list can go on and on. The German company Adidas sources most of its products from Asia. In China, it looks for potential suppliers who will either be very innovative, or be able to deliver high quality products in big volumes and at very low prices. Germans hate product returns. So Adidas has in its German headquarters a team of experts whose only job is to go visit the new supplier's facility, and sit with its management to help them drive efficiency in their production and supply chain in order to accommodate the business.

Bottom line: Before sending your sales team to knock on that multinational's door, be aware of what you're getting into.

让潜在客户接受你的会面请求

现在既然你已经会辨识目标客户，并且准备好了与他们进行第一次交锋，那么应该如何确保顺利与客户约定会面且不会遭拒呢？

提示1：这是一次客户开发，而不是陌生拜访

有时想要克服拿起电话拨通某个电话号码的恐惧是很困难的，尤其是和一位从未见过面的买家直接通话。这也是为什么有些公司会以发送电子邮件的方式代替电话沟通，但销售邮件其实毫无用处。那些曾经尝试通过电子邮件销售产品或服务的人也都知道这个道理。在你向一个素不相识的人发送电子邮件或拨打电话商定会面之前，请确保你在交谈过程中不会惊慌。你需要在几秒钟之内说出你打电话的目的，然后介绍你是谁。要按照这个顺序介绍，不能反过来。很多人错在一开始先讲他们是谁，结果很快被打断，根本没有

Securing a sales meeting with the prospect

Now that you have identified your target customer, and got ready to engage with them for the first time, how should you go about securing a meeting with the customer without being rejected?

Pointer1: It' s an exploration call, not a blind call

It is sometimes difficult to overcome the fear of picking up the phone and placing that call, especially if it's directed to a buyer with whom we have never met. That's why some companies elect to send an email instead. Sales emails are worthless. Those who have tried to sell their products or services through emails already know that. Before you send that email or place that call to ask for a meeting with a person you don't know, make sure you have the elements needed to not panic during the exchange. You should be able to say in a few seconds why you are calling first, then who you are. In that order, not the other way around. Many make the mistake of first saying who they are, but get interrupted quickly and don't have time to say why they are calling.

Imagine a call starting with "Hello, my name is Alicia, and I'm the general manager of Bright Future company that specializes in furniture. I am calling you

时间介绍他们打电话的目的。想象一下，一个电话这样开始："您好，我的名字叫艾莉莎，我是光明公司的总经理，我们专注做家具。我给您打电话是因为……"艾莉莎说了她是谁，但是她可能在完成自我介绍之前就被打断了。

现在想象这个电话开始于："您好，我是艾莉莎。我听说你们从中国进口家具的业务因为开始执行新关税而受到一些影响。我给您打电话是想分享下我们是如何成功帮助几个客户解决这个问题的。"这两个版本哪个更好？毫无疑问是第二个。

先告诉我你打电话的目的，以此来吸引我，再告诉我你是谁。

理想状态下，你最好已经在领英、微博或者其他地方做过一些调查，并且已确认过这位需要电话沟通的客户的身份。给一家公司拨打电话最好的方式向来都是"您好，我希望能够和你们采购部门的负责人约翰先生通话"，而不是"您好，我们是卖咖啡机的，我想和你们公司里对咖啡机感兴趣的人通话"。

提示 2：不要轻易告诉别人"我一直都有空"

把日程表放到面前，准备好两到三个时间空当以便安排会面。两到三个就行，不用太多。即使你下周的日程表是空的，也不要让你的潜在客户知道。如果一个销售代表打电话告诉我他下周的任何时间都有空，那么我便会自然而然地认为他没有其他事可做也没有其他客户要见，他的公司可能迫切需要生意。销售代表不应该让别人觉得自己渴望生意。你去参加展会或联谊会时也应该带上日程表。如果你碰到了一个可能成为潜在客户的人，立刻定下会面时间，然后再在不久的将来探索进一步合作的可能性。

because..." Alicia is saying who she is, but she might get interrupted before she finishes introducing herself.

Now consider the same call starting with "Hi, this is Alicia. I heard about the new tariffs imposed by your country on furniture products imported from China. I'm calling to explain to you how we are helping several businesses overcome those barriers today." Which one of the two versions resonates better? No doubt it's the 2nd version.

First tell me the purpose of your call to get me hooked, then tell me who you are.

Ideally, you would have already done some research on LinkedIn or Weibo or somewhere else, and confirmed the identity and position of the person you will need to call to secure a meeting. It's always better to call a company and say "Hello, I would like to talk to the head of your sourcing department Mr. John", rather than saying "Hello, we sell coffee machines and I would like to talk to someone at your company who might be interested in buying coffee machines".

Pointer2: Don' t tell everyone how empty your agenda is

Have your agenda open in front of you so you are ready to offer two or three time slots that would be convenient for you to meet. Two or three, no more. Even if your agenda is empty for the next week, do not let your prospect know about it. If a sales representative calls me and says he is free to meet any time next week, I will automatically assume that he has nothing else to do and no other prospects to meet. His company is probably desperate for business. No sales representative should sound desperate for a business. Your agenda should also follow you when you go to fairs or networking events. If you meet someone who might be a potential customer, secure a meeting right there and then to further explore opportunities in the near future.

Pointer3: Doing your homework in advance is very important

In a perfect world, before calling a prospect to ask for a meeting, you

提示 3：提前做好功课很重要

理想的状况是，在你致电潜在客户商定一次会面之前，已经准备好一些能在很短的时间内吸引该潜在客户注意的信息。比如“您好，是韦思先生吗？我是阿道，我听闻您计划在下个月扩大您的仓储空间，给您打电话是因为我们的仓储设备的价格非常有竞争力。您这周是否有空可以与我们进行一次会面呢……”

记住，类似这样的电话，其目的是促成这次会面，而非销售。想想什么可以提起对方的兴趣，让其答应与你而不是你的竞争者会面。

提示 4：转介绍客户非常有意义

多年来我用过的最好的方式是转介绍。如果一个朋友告诉我他刚好认识某个在我的目标列表中的某一家公司上班的人，我就会询问我的朋友是否可以用他的名义来联系该公司，回答基本上都是“当然可以”。在这种情况下，我打电话时一般这样起头：“您好，我叫阿道，是东方海默信息咨询有限公司的产品经理。我的好朋友 Apple Xu 推荐我与您聊聊贵公司 2016 年的计划。我衷心希望可以与您就 ×× 进行一次对话，请问您是否有空与我们会面交谈呢？”不需要问候“最近过得怎么样？”或“您方便讲话吗？”社交细节可以稍后再聊。

这个方法听起来或许显而易见，不过我可以告诉你，我收件箱里有很多电子邮件并不是这样开头的。

我喜欢尽可能多地用转介绍的方式。我喜欢在电话中这样开场：“早上好，珍妮，我是阿道。你的朋友勃博告诉我可以跟您聊一聊关于培训……”

would already have some piece of information that you can use to get the prospect's attention in the first few seconds. For example, "Hello, Mr. Wayne? I'm Abdelhak and I heard you have plans to extend your warehouse space next month. I thought I would call to tell you a bit about the warehouse facilities equipment we offer at competitive prices. What would your thoughts be on having an initial conversation with us sometimes this week about..."

Remember, the purpose of similar calls is to secure the meeting, not to sell. Think of what is going to intrigue the person on the phone to agree to meet with you versus meeting with a competitor.

Pointer4: Using customer referrals always makes sense

My best approach has been for years the referral approach. If a friend tells me they know someone who works at a specific company that happens to be on my target list, I would ask my friend if it is OK to contact the company on his behalf. The answer is generally "of course". In that instance, my call would start with something like "Hello, my name is Abdelhak Benkerroum, and I'm the product manager for Eastheimer International. My close friend Apple Xu suggested I talk with you about your company's plans for 2016. I would love to have an initial conversation with you about × ×. When is a good time for us to meet and talk?" No need for the "How are you?", and no need for "Are you free to talk?" Social niceties can wait until later.

This may sound obvious, but I can point you to many emails in my inbox that didn't start that way.

I like to use referrals as much as possible. I like my calls to start with something like this: "Hey, good morning, Jenny. My name is Abdelhak. Your friend Bob told me I can call you regarding the trainings..."

8 条守则打造完美第一印象

现在你已经与潜在客户约定了一次会面。你将于下周三与他进行第一次会面并且也已经为保障谈判的成功做好了万全的准备。那么在你走进潜在客户的办公室时，要注意些什么呢？

约定好见面是个不错的开始，不过留给你展示的时间依然有限。你需要遵从下面 8 条守则来给你的潜在客户留下完美的第一印象。通常来说，第一印象往往就是永久性的印象。这就意味着“走进房间”的时刻是你大展光彩的唯一机会。因此，如果你在起初的几分钟之内表现不佳，就很难再去弥补。

要想销售你的产品，你需要先销售自己。必须让你的潜在客户喜欢你并且乐于与你交谈和分享有价值的信息。他的第一反应和我们第一次与某个陌生人见面时的反应没有差别。这种反应是在问两个基本的问题：

- 我能相信这个人吗？
- 我能信任这个人的能力吗？

The 8 rules of a great first impression

You have secured a meeting with a potential customer. You are meeting next Wednesday for the first time and you have done all the preparation needed to make this negotiation a successful one. What should you keep in mind when walking into the prospect's office?

Securing an appointment is a good first step, and now you will have a limited time to play your magic. There are 8 rules you will need to abide by to make a great first impression of your potential customers. It is said that the first impression is always a lasting impression. That makes the "entering the room" phase your only chance to shine. If you mess up the first few minutes, it will be hard to make it up.

In order to sell your product, you will first need to sell yourself. The prospect must like you and feel comfortable talking with you and sharing valuable information. His first reaction will be that of any reaction we have when we meet a stranger for the first time. And that reaction is to ask two fundamental questions:

■ Can I trust this person?

下面我就为你介绍如何为成功通过接受度考验做好准备。

很多销售人员会额外做一件事，即在会议开始前几个小时打电话与潜在客户确认会面是否能正常进行。千万别这么做！如果你在明天下午两点有个会面，那么只要在两点准时出现就行。你不必在那天早上再打电话或发送邮件去确认已经约定好的会面。如果你打了电话，该客户便会找出 100 个理由来推迟会面。他们会告诉你他们正忙或者他们有另外的一个会议，甚至还会说来了个 VIP 访客。你还是直接在他们的办公室现身比较好，如果他们不在，给他们的接待员留言说你已经按约定时间赴会但没有见到他们。这不仅会给他们压力还会让他们因为羞愧而重新安排第二次会面。如果他们没能如约参加第一次会面，往往会抱有歉意并且会确保在第二次会面时如约而至。

现在就让我们来谈谈“走进房间”这一阶段的 8 条守则。

守则 1：着装得体

对于着装你应该三思而后行。如果你是与一家金融机构谈判，那么你就必须穿正装并搭配领带。如果对方是一家 IT 初创公司，那你不佩戴领带也无妨。着装的守则就是要与你前去的机构或者文化相衬。如果你是一位女士，穿一套略显性感的衣服出现在中东地区的公司里，将会给你的潜在客户传递错误的信号。

守则 2：随身携带一个笔记本

参加会议时随身携带一个笔记本已经成为我的一个习惯。无论是与潜在客户、公司老板还是你的团队成员见面，你都可以带上它。打开笔记本

■ Can I respect this person's capabilities?

The coming pages will prepare you to pass that first acceptability test successfully.

Many sales people go an extra step and call the prospect a few hours before the meeting to confirm the appointment. Never do that! If you have an appointment for tomorrow at 2pm, just show up at 2pm. You don't have to call or send an email in the morning to confirm an appointment that has already been confirmed. If you call, the prospect will find 100 reasons to postpone the meeting. They will explain to you that they are busy or they have another important meeting, or a VIP visitor. You'd better just show up at their office, and if they are not there, leave a message with the receptionist saying that you came to the meeting as agreed but they were not there. That will put pressure on them and shame them to reschedule a second meeting. If they ditched you on the first meeting, it is likely that they will feel apologetic and make sure they are there for the second one.

Now let us talk about the 8 rules of the "entering the room" phase.

Rule 1: Dress to impress

The way you dress should be thought of carefully. If your meeting is a financial institution, then you must wear a suite and a tie. If you are meeting with an IT startup, then not wearing the tie is OK. The rule here is to try to fit within the organization you are visiting, or the culture you are in. If you are a lady and wear even a slightly sexy outfit in Middle-East, you will be sending the wrong message to your prospect.

Rule 2: Show up with a notebook

I have made it a habit to never ever show up to a meeting without a notebook.

做笔记可以向坐在对面的客户传递出你不仅对其所谈的信息很感兴趣还很重视他的信息。即使有时候我们的团队里已经有一位专门的记录员，我也会确保自己在做记录。笔记本可以派上用场的另外一种情况是在谈判遭遇令人尴尬的沉默的时候。沉默也是一项可以在谈判中用到的有力技巧，这点我们稍后讨论。但当沉默变得尴尬时，你只要低头看你的笔记本，保持整理笔记的状态即可。

守则 3：带上你真诚的笑容

作为一名销售人员，你的工作就是广开思路以及打开客户的钱包。你要确保自己在这么做的时候始终带有真诚的微笑，谈吐自信。你必须以足够健康的方式表现出你的机敏、能干和有趣。语气要热情，保持眼神交流，展现积极的肢体语言。

守则 4：善待“绊脚石”

“绊脚石”指的是所有阻挡在你和潜在客户之间的人。他可能是客户办公室外面的保安、接待员、行政助理等。请确保每次你给潜在客户或客户送促销礼品、糖果的时候，都留一些给他们。这些人都能帮你获得机会，因为在许多公司中行政助理通常掌管着经理的日程表。他既能同意你的会面也能取消它，他还可以告诉你经理正在哪儿出差、和谁在一起等。

我想在这里讲述我在迪拜的一位客户的接待员安娜的例子。我每次都在会议开始前几分钟到场。在等待客户时我既不看我的笔记也不玩手机，我选

Being it a meeting with a prospect, a boss, or a team member. Opening a notebook and taking notes shows the prospect sitting in front of me that I am interested and that what he says matters to me. Even if we happen to have a dedicated note-keeper in our team, I make sure I take notes too. Another situation where the notebook comes in handy is when there is an awkward silence during the negotiation. Silence is a powerful technique that can be used against you during the negotiation and we will discuss it later. When the silence feels awkward, just get down on your notebook and keep organizing your notes.

Rule 3: Wear your authentic smile

Your job as a sales representative is to open minds and to open wallets. Make sure you do so all while smiling genuinely and carrying yourself in a confident manner. You must be healthy enough to look alert, capable and interested. Use an enthusiastic tone, maintain eye contact, and display a positive body language.

Rule 4: Be nice to the "barriers"

A "barrier" is every person that separates you from your prospects. It could be the security guard outside the prospect's office, the receptionist, the admin assistant…Make sure every time you bring promotional gifts or candies to the prospect or the customer, to save a few for them. These are the people who can help you get access, because generally the admin assistant is in charge of the manager's agenda in many companies. He can grant you a meeting, cancel it, tell you where the manager is travelling, who he is with…

I like to relate the example of one of my customer's receptionists in Dubai called Anna. I always showed up to meetings a few minutes in advance. Instead of reading my notes or playing with my phone while waiting for the customer, I took advantage of that time to chat with her. I have always valued the job of receptionists

择利用这段时间和她聊天。我向来重视接待员的工作，因为他们就是公司的门面。试想，让一个不匹配的人担任这项工作你就会明白，这将会对你的公司造成多大的伤害。

有一天我走进那个客户的公司并向接待员问好："嗨，安娜！最近工作怎么样？"她答道："太忙了，因为我们在自贸区新开了一家分部。"这简直是我那天获得的最有价值的信息！之后我走进办公室，与该名客户座谈了一个多小时。不出意料，他对他们自贸区的分部只字未提。一离开他们公司，我就径直驱车前往自贸区，搜集了关于那个分部的一切信息。

请记住：**每个人都很重要，**无论是清洁工还是最高管理者。

守则 5：正确打招呼

在有些文化里，人们打招呼的时候喜欢鞠躬而非握手。无论你所处什么样的文化之中，一定要对你的潜在客户所处的文化环境做足功课，并尽可能地贴近他的文化。如果你要握手，请确保你的力度（不要太使劲或太无力）。有一次我向一位首次见面的美国客户伸手问好，而他并没有伸手与我相握，那几秒钟我着实尴尬。后来我了解到，他是因为有手掌多汗症（表现为手掌过度出汗的医学症状）而不好意思和我握手。此时的守则便是不要先伸手，而是等对方发起握手动作。如果他们没有行动，你可以轻微点头以示问好。

在你握手的时候，注意握手的状态。手掌略微倾斜且手心向上表示对方欢迎你并且可能顺从你，手心向下代表权力和控制。不过请注意，女士或许会以手心向下的方式握手，但并不表示她是支配者。

because they are the voice and the face of the company. Put an incompetent person there and see how this will hurt your business.

One day I walked into their office and greeted her "Hey Anna, how is work these days?", to which she answered "Very busy with the new branch office we are opening in the free zone". That was the most valuable information I had that day! Not surprisingly, after I went in, I sat down with the customer and chatted for over an hour. He didn't mention a word about their free zone branch. But as soon as I left their office, I drove straight to the free zone to glean whatever information I could about that office.

Remember that **everybody is important**. From the cleaning lady up to the top manager.

Rule 5: Greet appropriately

Some cultures favor bowing rather than hand-shaking. Whichever culture you are in, do your homework by searching cultural aspects of your prospect and adapting as close as you could. If you shake hands, make sure the handshake is firm (not crushing or limp). I once extended my hand to greet an American client I was meeting for the first time, and he didn't extend his hand back to shake mine. Those few seconds I felt really awkward. I learned later on that he was embarrassed to shake my hand because he suffered from palmar hyperhidrosis, a medical condition that is characterized by excessive sweating of the hands. The rule here is not to extend your hand first but wait for the other party to initiate the handshake. If they don't, you can use a small head-nod as a greeting.

When you shake hands, notice how the handshake develops. A handshake where his hand is slightly tilted with a palm up means he is welcoming and maybe submissive. A handshake where the palm is facing down displays authority and dominance. Be aware that a female might shake hands with a palm facing down and still not be perceived as dominant.

守则 6：验证身份

你是否曾走进一个人的办公室，打过招呼并简单聊过后才发现你走错了房间，与错误的人进行了交谈？我就有过这样的经历。为防止这种情况再次发生，我会在见到潜在客户的第一时间就验明他们的身份。一句“您好，请问您是克里斯·丹尼尔森先生吗？”就可以让你免遭尴尬。说出姓氏和名字时需咬字清晰，因为在同一个公司里可能会有好几个克里斯或者吉米。另外一个方法是在你见到潜在客户的第一时间递上你的名片，他们见状自然也会分享他们的名片。那时你便可以看到他们的姓名和职位，也就能够确保没有走错房间了。

Rule 6: Validate the identity

Have you ever walked into someone's office, greeted and engaged in a small talk, to realize a few seconds later that you have entered the wrong room and started talking to the wrong person? It happened to me. To prevent this from occurring again, once I meet the prospect, I validate their identity. Something like "Hi, are you Mr. Kris Danielson?" could save you some embarrassment. Pronounce both the first name and the last name clearly. One same company could have several Kris's or Jimmy's. Another way to do it is to present your business card as soon as you meet with the prospect. They will feel compelled to replicate and share theirs. You will then be able to see their name and job title and make sure you didn't enter the wrong meeting room.

守则 7：不要第一个坐下

有一次，我走进一位客户的办公室，他和我握了手并让我坐下。安排我坐好后，他穿过办公桌，站在一块白板前一边在上面写字一边对我讲话。我感觉自己就像是一个正在听课的学生，或是警察局里一名正在被审问的犯罪嫌疑人。某个时刻，在我感觉到他在主导时，我站起来，走到白板前对他说："这是个不错的点。请问您是否介意我也在白板上写下我的观点？"他同意了，我也真的这么做了，于是我就一直站在他跟前完成了后半部分的讨论。

不管你怎么看，如果一个人所处的位置比你高，那么他的优势也会胜你一筹，这是权势和力量的表现。它发生在当你坐着而另一个人站着，或者你站着而另一个人坐在更高的地方时。这也是为什么法官坐的法桌位于一个高置的平台。即使是站起来进行庭审发言的律师，也无法压制坐在高处的法官。

万一碰到潜在客户想让你坐下，而你却不希望先坐，你只要把公文包放在椅子上即可。你可以假装正在找你的笔记本、书或是手提电脑。这个动作可以给你几秒钟的时间来观察那名潜在客户是否已经走到一边并且坐下。

守则 8：喝水无忧

如果对方问你想喝什么，回答喝水即可。有些文化中人们的习惯是喝茶，所以如果对方给你沏茶，也别拒绝。但是在你可以从水、可乐、茶以及咖啡中进行选择时，要选择喝水，因为有些公司真的做不好咖啡。想想

Rule 7: Don’t be the first to sit down

I once walked into a customer’s office. He shook my hand and led me to the chair, then offered me to sit down. Once he sat me down, he moved across the table, stood in front of a white board, and started talking to me while scribbling over the board. I felt like I was a little student being lectured by a teacher or a suspect being questioned by a cop in a police station. At some point, when I started feeling his dominance, I stood up, walked over to the board and said: “That’s a valid point. Do you mind if I write on the board too so you see how I think this idea will develop?” He agreed, so I did, and I stayed there standing in front of him for the rest of the discussion.

No matter how you look at it, if a person’s position is more elevated than yours, then that person has an edge over you. It displays dominance and power. It could be a person standing while you are sitting, or a person sitting at an elevated location while you are standing. That’s why judges sit in a raised platform called the Bench. Even if a lawyer stands to make a case, he will not overpower the judge who sits at an elevated spot.

In case a prospect offers you to sit down and you want him to sit first, just put your briefcase over the chair, and pretend you are reaching for your notebook, your book, or your laptop. That will give you a few seconds to find out if the prospect has already moved over to the other side and sat down.

Rule 8: Water never fails you

If asked what to drink, just go for the water. It is normal to offer tea in some cultures, and if you are offered a tea, do not decline. If however you are offered to choose between water, a Coke, tea, or coffee, then go for the water. Some companies just don’t know how to make a good coffee. Imagine taking a sip from your coffee

你才啜一小口咖啡就面目狰狞的样子吧！你的潜在客户自然能明白并会感到尴尬。选择喝水的话你就可以避免这种情况的发生，因为至少我们都知道水是什么味道。

我不建议你在他们提供饮品时说“谢谢，不用了”。因为在谈判过程中如果出现令人尴尬的沉默，而你并不想打破时，手上有杯饮品，你就可以喝上几口以争取点时间。

我在这个章节开始的时候讲过，你的潜在客户对你的第一印象与你给每一个陌生人的第一印象是一样的。这个第一印象会回答我们两个基本问题：我信任这个人吗？我认可这个人的能力吗？

即使你拥有这个世界上最棒的产品、服务、想法，对方不信任你，你也永远得不到他们的订单。信任是一把钥匙。

在我 16 岁的时候，我的一个好友让我借给他 200 美元，帮助他解决一些个人问题。那个时候我还很年轻，这笔钱相当于我的全部积蓄，但我还是借给了他，因为我们相互认识且常常见面。这位朋友承诺他将会在一周后归还这笔钱。一个星期过去了，他没有还钱。我给他打电话，他请求我多给他几天时间筹钱，我同意了。一周后，我再打电话给他，他既没有接电话也没有回信息。

我尝试联系了他好几次，但都没找到他。我之后再也没有见到过这个人。我的电话和信息都石沉大海，这个朋友消失了。那一天，我告诫自己以后再也不要相信任何人。

很多年过去了，我花了好长时间才意识到生活中是不可能没有信任的。想象一下你的生活中，你不信任一起工作的同事，一起生活的丈夫/妻子，一起出去玩的朋友，这绝对是难以忍受的生活。

那个时候我自问：“信任到底是什么？”除了生意之外，离开了信任，生

and wincing! The prospect will automatically pick up the signal and will feel embarrassed. You can avoid that by ordering water because we all know how water tastes like most of the time.

I wouldn't recommend to say "thank you, nothing" when offered a drink. That drink can come in handy when you have a moment of awkward silence during the negotiation, and you don't want to break that silence... It's a good moment to take a sip to buy a few more seconds.

I said at the beginning of this section that the first reaction of the prospect when they see you for the first time will be that of any reaction we have when we meet a stranger for the first time. And that reaction is to ask ourselves two fundamental questions: Can I trust this person? Can I respect this person's capabilities?

You can have the most amazing product/service/idea in the world. If the other party doesn't trust you, you will never secure their business. Trust is key.

When I was 16 years old, a close friend of mine asked me to lend him 200 USD to help him overcome some personal situation. I was young at that time, and that amount represented almost all my savings. But I accepted to lend him that money anyways because we knew each other and we met regularly. That friend promised he will return that money to me after one week. One week passed by, and he didn't return it, so I called him and asked him to give me back the money he borrowed from me. He asked me to grant him an extra few days to gather that cash, and I agreed. A week later I called him to ask for my money but he didn't pick up my calls nor answer my messages. I tried several times to reach him but it was impossible. I never heard from that guy again. My calls and messages were left unanswered, and that friend disappeared. That day, I promised myself that I will never ever trust anyone in my life.

Years passed, and it took me some time to realize that it was impossible to live a life without trust. Imagine you are living a life where you don't trust the people you work with, the husband/wife you live with, the friends you hang out with. It's an unbearable life.

活是会无以为继吗？如何建立信任？如何维持信任？它真的可以从零开始建立吗？尤其是当你合作的那些外国买家还是坐在世界另一边的电脑前的情况下。要知道，那个外国人从来没有见过你，没有收到过你的货物，但他不得不敲下那个付款键。

你如何在商业环境下建立信任？如何跟你的客户、合作方、供应商、权威人士等建立信任？

- 从你的员工开始。作为一名经理，如果你关注员工，他们就会关注客户。如果你公平正直地帮助你的员工，他们也会这样对待客户。你作为一名管理者，是公司的门面。
- 正直是做对的事情，即使没有人注意。让我再次重复这句话：正直是做对的事情，即使没有人注意。例如一个客户多付了钱，但他们没有意识到，在他们意识到错误并跟你要钱**之前**把钱还给他们。
- 跟对方建立情感链接。你不需要通过去朋友圈点赞的方式建立友谊。你要让他们知道他们正在跟一个真正的人合作，而不是面无表情的机器。公司无法跟公司合作，是人和人在合作。建立情感链接的机会每天都有，包括你在邮件中的照片、打电话、见面。生意是人的体验，邀请你的合作方、供应商、客户来拜访你、见你、熟悉你。这是我们建立有意义的关系的关键所在。
- 同理心。把你自己放进对方的角色里。**听着！**展示你对客户的兴趣，而不是试图拿到他们的生意。买家并不仅仅是买，他们把情感的部分也加进来了。销售人员和产品在客户心目当中是不可分割的。如果你想提高你的同理心，那就去做公益活动，它是最好的同理心老师。因为在公益项目中，那些真正因你受益的人不会关注你多么有钱或多么

So at that moment I asked myself: "What is trust?" Beyond business, is it possible to live a life without trusting others? How to establish trust? How to maintain it? Can it actually be built from scratch, especially in contexts where you deal with a foreign buyer sitting in front of his laptop on the other side of the world. That foreigner has never seen you, has not received your goods, yet he has to click on that button to make that deposit payment.

So how can you build trust in a business community? Trust with clients, partners, suppliers, authorities, and so forth.

- Start from your own people. If you are a manager, and you care about your employees, they will care about your clients. If you treat your employees with fairness and integrity, they will treat the client with fairness and integrity. You, the manager, are the face of trust for your company.
- Integrity is doing the right thing even when no one is looking. Let me repeat this one again: Integrity is doing the right thing even when no one is looking. If a client over-pays you, and they don't realize it, give them their money back BEFORE they realize their mistake and ask for a refund.
- Build emotional connections with others. You don't build friendships with others by going to their social media and giving them thumbs-ups. Show others that they are dealing with a real person, not a faceless corporate logo. Companies don't do business with companies. People do business with people. Every time you get a chance, include your picture in your emails, place that phone call, go out and meet face to face with that person. Business is a human experience. Invite your business partners, suppliers, clients to come visit you, see you, and feel you. That's how we build meaningful relationships.
- Empathy: Immerse yourself in other's perspective. LISTEN! Show interest in your clients instead of trying to get their interest. Buyers don't just buy, they enter a relationship. The seller and the product are inseparable in the

出名，他们只关注你对他们有多少同理心。

- 成为你自己。坚持自我，不要把真正的自己隐藏起来。如果你这么做，你就很难得到信任。在一段关系建立之初，说了什么比做了什么更重要，因为在此之前你从来没有看到我做过什么事情。随着时间的推移，我的行为突显出来，我言语的意义越来越小而行动的意义越来越大。坚持自我意味着言行一致。

  一个坚持自我的人会说："先生，非常抱歉，我们犯了一些错误导致没办法赶上产品的最后期限。这是因为……这是我们接下来能做的补救措施……这是我们为了防止类似事情发生将会采取的行动……"

- 谅解。一些你信任的人可能会辜负你的信任，无论如何要信任别人，谅解那些辜负你的人。这样做不是因为他们值得你的谅解，而是因为这是唯一一个让你释怀，也让别人释怀的选择。

根据我多年的销售经验，我把客户分成 3 种类别：

- 不满意客户：这是敌人。他想要伤害你并很享受这个过程。你跟他道歉或者不道歉都没有关系。不满意客户不会常常跟你抱怨，他们只会转身离开并把生意带到别处。他们还会告诉他们的朋友、家人和同事。把他们的不良体验放到他们的社交平台上。而且悲哀的是，一个国外采购商不会说"这个供应商很差"，他们只会说"这个中国制造的产品很差"。
- 满意客户：客户满意并不意味着一切，因为满意只是一种感觉、一种情绪，而情绪是波动的。这个客户今天高兴，明天有可能不高兴。满意客户并不爱你，如果别的地方有更好的生意，他们就会离开。
- 忠诚客户：忠诚客户会说，"你是我的供应商，我不在乎其他地方是不是有比你更好的。我不会换供应商，我只跟你合作，你会给我我所需

client's mind. If you want to improve your empathy, do charity work. It's the best teacher of empathy. Because people who benefit from your charity don't care how rich you are or how famous you are. They just care about how empathetic you are to them.

- Be YOU. Be authentic. Don't hold back who you are. If you do, you are less likely to be trusted. At the beginning of a relationship, what I say to you seems more important than what I do, because you have never seen me doing anything before. With time, my behavior becomes apparent, and my words mean less but my actions mean more. Being authentic means your words and your actions are the same.

An authentic person says "Mr. Customer, I'm sorry we made some mistakes and we won't be able to meet the production deadline. Here is the reason why. Here is what we will do to fix this. Here is what we will do to prevent it from happening again."

- Forgiveness: Some people you trust will breach that trust. Trust others anyways. Forgive those who breached your trust. Not because they deserve it, but because that is the only thing that will set you free, and set them free. In the course of my years in business, I came to deal with 3 types of customers:
- Unhappy customer: That's the enemy. He wants to hurt you and he enjoys it. It doesn't matter if you apologize to him or not. Unhappy customers don't always complain to you, they just leave and take their business elsewhere. AND they tell their friends and family and coworkers. AND advertise their bad experience on their social media. And the sad part is that a foreign buyer won't say "This supplier is bad". They would say "This Made in China product is bad".
- Satisfied customer: A satisfied customer doesn't mean anything because happiness is a feeling, an emotion. And emotions fluctuate. Today that

要的。如果你的竞争对手拿一个特别有吸引力的报价找我，我会拿给你看，然后问问你能做些什么跟他竞争”。

如何得到忠诚客户？很简单。客户忠诚度意味着信任。如果我信任你，我就会对你忠诚。

中国丽思卡尔顿酒店在几年前做过一个调查来分析他们的忠诚客户在说爱这家酒店的时候意味着什么。他们发现当一位客户说爱这家酒店时，是在说这家酒店让他感觉像在家里，像在妈妈的家里，生活可以随心所欲。当有什么事情不对劲时，你跑去找妈妈，她永远不会说“让我给经理打个电话”，她会说“来吧，我就在这里照顾你，我是因为你才在这里的。”

这就是怎样让客户对你有好感并形成对你的看法。如果你对他们友好，表现出对他们很在乎，他们在跟你买东西之前，就已经对你形成了一定的看法。每一次跟客户的互动都是客户服务。这就是我持续不断地告诉销售员们“客户服务不是一个部门，而是一种态度”的原因。这种态度开始于客户跟你联系时前 5 秒的观察。如果客户给你打电话，电话响了三次以上才被接起，客户会觉得被忽视。客户进入你的停车场时，他在看到你的厂房外观的时候就已经对你形成了看法。他们都还没有跟你说话，但是已经对你形成了看法。

如果你想知道客户是怎么看待你的，问他！

■ 问你的客户，如果按 1 到 10 来打分的话，他们会给你的产品打多少分。如果他们说 7，问他：“我们如何提高到 9、10 呢？”

■ 问你的客户要推荐。你可以问他，“你跟我们做生意觉得开心吗？”如果他说开心，接着问他，“在你的圈子里，有没有你也想让他们开心的

customer is happy, but tomorrow he is not. A satisfied customer does not love you. If there is better deal somewhere else, that's where they will go do their business.

■ Loyal customer: The loyal customer says "You are my supplier and I don't care if there is anything better somewhere else. I will not move somewhere else but I will work with you so you can give me what I need. And if your competitor approaches me with an amazing offer, I will take it, show it to you, and ask you how you can match it."

How can you reach that level of loyalty in your business? It's simple. Customer loyalty means trust! I will be loyal to you if I trust you.

The Hotel chain Ritz Carlton carried a survey a few years ago to understand what their loyal customers meant when they said they loved that hotel. The Ritz Carlton people found out that when a customer said he loved the hotel, it was because it felt like home. It meant that the customer felt like at his mom's place. Life is like the way he wanted it. When something goes wrong and you go to your mom, she never says "Let me call the manager." She says"Come, I'm here to take care of you, I'm here for you."

That's how customers feel good with you, and that's how they build an opinion about you. If you are nice to them, and show that you care, before they even buy from you, they have already built their opinion about you. Every interaction with the customer is customer service. That's why I keep telling businesses "Customer service is not a department. It's an attitude". And that attitude starts the moment the customer perceives they made contact with you. It doesn't start 5 seconds later. If the customer calls you and the phone rings more than 3 times, then that customer feels ignored. If the customer enters your parking lot, his subconscious is already building an opinion about you just by looking at the outside of your building. They didn't talk to you yet but they have already formed an opinion of you.

If you want to know what opinion your client has of you, ask him!

人？”如果他们的答案是肯定的，并且推荐给你了，那基本上就意味着他们信任你了。

5 年前，我来到中国，四处寻找可以出口到海外的产品。我发现，当我走进一个城市想要采购一个商品的时候，有超过 1,000 家工厂都在生产基本上一模一样的商品。我因此很纠结可以信任哪一家工厂，可以跟哪一家工厂做生意。开始的时候，选择对我来讲非常困难，但是我接受了风险，信任其实就是接受风险。

- Ask your client on a scale from 1 to 10, how much do they trust your product? If they say 7, ask them "How can we bring that to 9, to 10?"
- Ask your clients for referrals. Ask them "Are you happy doing business with us?" If they are, ask them "Do you know someone from your circle that you want to make happy too?" If their answer is yes, and they recommend you, it generally means that they trust you.

Five years ago, I arrived in China and traveled around looking for products to buy and export overseas. It happened to me that I went to a city looking into buying a commodity, and found that over 1,000 factories in that city are producing the exact same commodity. So I asked myself which factory can I trust with my business, and which one I can do business with. It was very hard for me to choose someone in the beginning. But I took risks. And trust is also about taking risks.

3 个步骤用闲聊开启正式谈判

不管是在一场销售会议还是一次联谊会上，你总会发现很难以闲聊的方式切入主题。有什么建议可以给那些因为担心被发现目的太明确而不知道如何开启对话的人呢?

在谈判开始前可以通过 3 个阶段开启非正式的讨论。它们分别是：闲聊阶段、时长评估阶段、过渡阶段。由于讨论的走向都很难预料，建议你在了解这些步骤的同时也关注对话开始后的具体语境。

阶段 1: 快速进入闲聊状态

闲聊对谈判结果的影响很大。其包括讨论一些一般性话题以便双方相互了解、建立信任并最终找到共同话题。这些一般性话题可以是对于墙上挂着的证书、谈判的地点、来谈判的路上发生的一件事的评论等。可以聊的话题数不胜数，不过建议你与那些可能产生摩擦的政治和宗教类话题保持距离。理想状况下，这个阶段是你和其他人建立关系的良好时机。

你也可以利用这个阶段，通过分享对该潜在客户或许有重要意义的信息来为自己创造价值。这些信息可以是发生在他们区域的某个事件，他们的竞争者发布新品的新闻或其他任何与他们有关的消息。

是否要开启一段闲聊可以依具体情况而定。有时潜在客户问你想喝什么，有时他会先让你坐到座位上。第一种情况更有利于闲聊。有时你们一起坐在沙发上，有时你们面对面坐在办公桌前，前者比后者的情况要更有利。

Transitioning from the informal to formal talk in three stages

Whether at a sales meeting or at a networking event, you always find it hard to open a discussion with a small talk before getting to the topic. What suggestions are there for those who don't know how to kick-off the discussion because they don't want to be perceived as too direct in the beginning?

There are three phases to follow in starting the informal discussion that takes place before the negotiation begins. Those are: the Small Talk phase, the Time Validation phase, and the Transition phase. While the way any discussion can go is rarely predictable, it is recommended to be aware of those steps and then be responsive to the context of the discussion when it begins.

Phase 1: Swiftly entering the Small Talk mode

Small Talk can have big influence on the negotiation's outcome. It consists of discussing general topics to get to know each other, build trust, and eventually find common ground. Those general topics could be a comment on the diplomas hanging on the wall, the location of the meeting, an event that took place on your way to the meeting , etc. There are countless topics to start a discussion with, but it is recommended to stay clear from topics that could create friction such us politics or religion. Ideally, this phase will be an opportunity to create a connection with the other party.

You can also use this phase for value creation by sharing information that might be of importance to the prospect. It could be about an event taking place in their area or a news of their competitor releasing a new product or anything of relevance.

Whether or not to engage in a "Small Talk" depends on the context. Does the prospect ask you what you would like to drink or does he direct you immediately to your chair? The first situation is more conducive to small talks. Are you sitting

有些销售代表喜欢马上进入谈判状态，这样开始也非常好。而我通常会先问一句“最近生意怎么样”。直接谈判这个方法唯一的缺点是你会错过进行时长评估的机会。

阶段 2: 时长评估

就像字面意思那样，时长评估的目的就是让你明确自己将在这个潜在客户身上花费多少时间，以便调整相应的谈话内容和策略。该潜在客户可能必须在 30 分钟内赶去开会，而你本来计划用一小时来辨识他的需求并给出建议。这个问题也可以通过询问“您今天可以留多长时间给我们”来解决。不过，潜在客户往往会给出一个时间但并不一定遵守。即使那样也无妨，只要你在开始问过并且对其他人的时间安排有过考虑就可以了。

阶段 3: 过渡

这个阶段在时长评估过后就会出现。如果潜在客户同意会面，他就已经大致知道你将会和他谈什么。不过一个好的过渡可以让你将谈话从闲聊转到话题核心。举个例子，可以这么说：“我们今天与您见面是想多了解一些你们的业务情况，看看我们的服务可以在哪些方面给您的生产流程带来速度和效率的提升。”正确地表述这样的过渡语句，就是在邀请潜在客户先谈他们的业务，这样一来你就可以回问相应的问题从而辨识他们的确切需求。

together on a couch or are you sitting at a desk across from each other? The first situation is more inviting than the latter.

Some sales representatives prefer to engage in a business talk right away, and there is no harm in that if it is done properly. I have started many discussions right after the greeting by asking "How is business going". The only drawback to that approach is that you will miss the opportunity to do a Time Validation.

Phase 2: The Time Validation

As it indicates, the Time Validation aims at identifying how much time you will spend with the prospect, which will allow you to adapt your content and your strategy. The prospect might have to leave for a meeting within 30 minutes, whereas you have planned to spend an hour identifying the needs and making proposals. This question could be asked simply by saying "How much time do you have available for us today". You will notice that more often than not, the prospect will say a time but will not necessarily stick to it. No harm in that, as long as you asked in the beginning and showed respect for the other party's time.

Phase 3: The Transition

This phase can come right after the Time Validation phase. If the prospect has accepted to come to a meeting, they already have an idea of what you will discuss, but a good transition would give you the opportunity to pivot the discussion from small talks to the core of the topic. For example, this could go something like "We wanted to meet with you today to learn a bit more about your business and see where our services could drive speed and efficiency into your production process". By framing that transition properly, you are inviting the prospect to start talking about their business first so you can fire back by asking the right questions to identify their exact needs.

把握谈判核心阶段，助力最终成交

一次理想的谈判是怎么从开启过渡阶段，到将话题引入核心部分，再到最终成交的呢？

理想谈判一般会经历三个主要阶段：需求辨析、出价和阻力应对。这些阶段有时会重叠，但是你有必要了解它们并知道如何应对。

需求辨析阶段是问问题以及建立认知的过程。一旦你对潜在客户的需求有了很好的了解，你就要根据这些需求进行**报价**。潜在客户并不会仔细听你给出的报价并告诉你"谢谢，我很喜欢，成交"，他们一定会想要更优惠的价格以及更好的条件。所以他们会提出一些需要你来正确应对的异议，该阶段被称为**阻力应对**阶段。

阶段 1：需求辨析

在这一阶段，你将通过一系列的问答来指引潜在客户确定基本需求。你将要尝试**帮助该潜在客户辨析其商业需求，或者让其了解他们的目标与现状的差距**。那么，你可以采取以下措施。

1. 交替使用开放式问题和封闭式问题。

封闭式问题是指可以用"是"或"否"来回答的问题。开放式问题则能引发更长的回答，一般以如何、为什么、何时、谁等字眼起头。开放式问题不仅可以用来搜集信息还能让你的潜在客户开口讲话。封闭式问题则用于认定事实和确认对方的理解程度。如果你的公司是物流公司，以下便是一个你可以用来辨析需求的例子：

Mastering the different negotiation phases to facilitate closing the deal

How would an ideal negotiation develop from the moment you initiate a transition to the heart of the topic to the moment you close the deal?

The ideal negotiation would go through three major phases: Needs Identification, Offer Making, and Objections Handling. Those phases will sometimes overlap. But it is necessary to be aware of them and the way they are handled.

The **Needs Identification** phase is all about asking questions and building understanding. Once the needs of the prospect are very well understood, you will have to **Make Offers** that will address those needs. No prospect will listen carefully to what you have to offer and say "Thank you. I like this. We have a deal." They will certainly want to negotiate a better pricing and better terms. So they will come up with objections that you will need to handle properly. And that phase is called the **Objections Handling** phase.

Phase 1: Needs identification

In this phase, you will take the prospect through a series of questions and answers to identify their requirements. You will try to **help the potential buyer to identify a business need, or a gap between where they are today and where they want to be in the future**. In order to do so, you need to:

1. Alternate open questions and closed questions.

Closed questions are questions that can be answered by either a "yes" or a "no". Open questions elicit longer responses, and start with How, Why, When, Who... Open questions are used to gather information and get the prospect talking. Closed questions are used to lock down facts and confirm understanding. If you are a logistics company, here is an example of questions you could ask to identify needs:

- 您当前在管理供应链方面正面临什么样的挑战？
- 您公司每月需运输多少吨货物？
- 目前哪家公司负责贵公司的物流业务，它们的附加值是什么？
- 您最想解决的物流方面的问题是什么？**（请注意，这个问题要紧跟你询问竞争者是谁的那个问题，其目的是让客户产生联想，即他当前的物流供应商需要在某处加以改善，而这方面的改善可能刚好是你的公司可以提供的。）**
- 您怎么看贵公司未来几个月的业务增长趋势？
- 针对这个特殊的服务，您的采购流程是什么？
- 为了拿到这个项目的完整信息，我需要跟你们公司的谁来沟通？
- 从 1 到 10 来打分的话，您对你们现有的供应链的满意程度如何？我们如何帮您把评分提高到 10？

2. 在会面时带上一份问卷或许可以帮你一个问题都不落地完成这个过程。

即使你对问卷不太感兴趣，也还是可以带上一份。在会前浏览一遍，可以确保自己不遗漏任何一个想要询问的主题。

3. 认真聆听。

在你的潜在客户说话时要做到认真聆听。你可能觉得这再正常不过，但你需要做的是表现出你真的在听。你可以通过在谈判期间做大量的记录并不时地点头来表示你在跟进。

4. 你也可以使用“我知道了”或者“噢、啊”等口头语。

验证和总结。由于不同的个性和背景，潜在客户在说某件事情的时候你可能会理解成其他事情，因此，你需要不时地验证该客户所说的话。你可以这么说：

- What kind of challenges are you facing currently in managing your supply chain?
- How many tons of shipments do you move per month?
- Who handles your logistics currently and what's their value-added?
- If there was one thing that you want to improve in the way your logistics is done, what would that be? **(notice here, this question comes right after you ask about your competition. The goal is to create a mental association in the customer's mind where you make him think his current logistics provider needs to improve somewhere. That improvement is what your company might be able to offer.)**
- How do you see your business growing in the coming months?
- What is your buying process for this specific service?
- Who else should I talk to within your company to get a full picture of this project?
- On a scale from 1 to 10, how satisfied are you today with your supply-chain processes? How can we work with you to bring that to 10?

2. Walk into the meeting with a questionnaire that could support you in the process so you don't leave any stone unturned.

If you are not a big fan of questionnaires, it is still worth preparing one that you can go through before walking into the meeting so you make sure you cover all topics you intended to cover.

3. Listen attentively.

This might seem obvious to you that you must listen to a prospect when he is talking. But you also have to demonstrate that you are really listening. To do so, take extensive notes during the meeting, and nod from time to time to show that you are not lost.

4. You can also use verbal cues such as "I see" or "uh huh".

Validate and summarize. Given the different personalities and backgrounds, the prospect will say something and you will understand something else. Every once and then, you will have to validate what the customer is saying. You can do so by stating:

■ 如果我的理解正确的话，您……

■ 对于这个，您的意思是……

■ 总结一下，您刚才说的是……

5. 别急着报价。

在聆听客户对你的问题的回答时，时刻想着你的产品或服务如何满足他提到的需求，但不要给出任何报价。你只需要让你的产品或服务与这些需求建立联系，以便通过这些信息核算价格。

请牢记需求辨析阶段并不总是你问一个问题潜在客户回答一个问题这种单向的谈话形式。如果是的话，这就该叫做采访阶段了。根据潜在客户的健谈程度，他也可能会问一些你能够简要回答的问题，而非出于索要报价的意图。你需要在给出一个完整的报价前做好全局规划，这意味着你需要在推进销售流程的过程中尽可能多地扩展谈话的层面。

阶段 2：不要让粗放式报价吓跑客户

当我还是法国马赛商学院（KEDGE）的年轻学生时，曾决定找一个暑期实习。最终一家小型软件和信息技术公司愿意雇用我做几周的销售工作。这家公司的两位老板人脉很广，他们手上有几个利润丰厚的合同，这既归功于他们公司出色的技术，也多亏了他们的人脉。他们的一位潜在客户是法国国家彩票公司（La Française des Jeux，FDJ），一家市值几十亿美元的上市公司。该公司的老板已经与 FDJ 有过好几轮的洽谈，并且安排了一次会议，准备提交最终提案。该提案涉及 FDJ 正计划在其分部开发和运营的一个软件。我们在一个周一下午和 4 位 FDJ 团队成员，同时也是该项目的决策者进行了

- If I understood properly, you…
- What you mean by this is…
- To summarize what you have just said…

5. Don't make that offer too quickly.

As you are listening to the customer answering your questions, keep thinking how your products or services will serve the needs he is mentioning. Don't make any offer yet. Just mentally link your products and services to the needs you uncovered. This will allow you to adapt your message later on when you are making your offer.

Keep in mind that the Needs Identification phase is not always a one-way conversation where you will be asking questions and the prospect will be answering them. If it was the case, it would be called The Interview phase. Depending on how talkative the prospect is, he might be asking you questions as well that you can answer briefly, without attempting to make an offer. You will need to have the full picture before making a consistent offer, and that means you will need to cover as many aspects as possible in your exchanges before you move on.

Phase2: Don't let your bulk offer scare away your prospect

I was a young student at the Marseille School of Business in France (KEDGE) when I decided to look for a summer internship. I found a small software and IT company that was willing to hire me for a few weeks to do Sales for them. The business owners were two well-connected guys who had landed a few juicy contracts thanks to their exceptional technical skills and, well, thanks also to their connections. One of their potential customers was La Française des Jeux (FDJ), a multi-billion Dollars public company. The business owners had already gone through a few rounds of discussions with FDJ, and had a meeting scheduled to submit a final proposal for a software that FDJ was planning to develop and

会面。讨论才进行了 5 分钟，其中一位 FDJ 团队成员，也是该项目的经理便打断我们说道：“你们为什么不先告诉我们这要花费多少钱，这样我们才可以在随后讨论细节问题。”于是我们的一位老板便回答说：“这是一份两年期的合同，一共将花费 150 万欧元，其中包括一……”话音未落他就被对方喊着“Sortezd' ici！”制止。“Sortezd' ici”翻译过来就是“滚出去”。我们本来以为他在开玩笑，但他又以更加强烈的语气重复了一次：“Non non，sortezd' ici！ Tout de suite！”意思是：“不，够了，离开这里！赶紧的！”我们用“这怎么可能”的表情互相看了看，并试着和他讲道理，但已经来不及了。剩下的几名 FDJ 团队成员告诉我们必须离开他们的办公室，别再浪费他们的时间了。我当时 21 岁，着实花了不少时间才消化了“这一课”的内容，回头再看，我才意识到发生了什么。

那天发生了什么?

这是在出价阶段出现问题的一个典型案例。如果你在这个节点处理不当，恢复元气就要付出很大的代价。就我们的团队而言，我们不仅失去了一笔 150 万欧元的潜在收入，还失去了未来与 FDJ 合作的巨大机遇。

在不涉及太多细节的情况下，我将在这里列出可以从上述交易中吸取的教训。

1. 别用整数定价。

如果你用一个整数定价，就会传递出你其实并不知道自己在做什么的信号。你有没有想过为什么超市的定价总是 5.99 美元，而不是 6 美元? 来自哥伦比亚大学商学院玛丽亚·梅森的一项调查显示：

“根据社会心理学的研究，相比整数，人们更愿意接受比其更精确的数字。”

潜在客户倾向于认为 9,650 美元的定价是经过你大量的计算和数据分析

implement in one of its divisions. We walked into the meeting one Monday afternoon to sit down with a team of four FDJ people who were the decision makers for that project. Five minutes into the discussion, one of FDJ's team members, the project manager, interrupted us and said "Why don't you tell us first how much this will cost us and we can go through the specifics afterwards." Hence, one of the two business owners said: "This will cost 1.5 Million Euros for a 2 years contract that includes a…" He was cut off by the project manager who snapped "Sortezd'ici!", which translates to "Get out of here!" We thought he was joking, but he repeated with a rather aggressive tone: "Non non, sortezd'ici! Tout de suite!", meaning "No, no, get out of here! Now!" We looked at each other with "This CAN'T be happening" looks, and tried to reason with him, but it was too late. We were told by the rest of FDJ team that we have to leave their office and do not waste their time again. I was 21 years old at that time, and it took me some time to learn from that lesson. Looking back at it, I realized what happened.

What happened there?

This story is a typical case of what could go wrong during the Offer Making phase. If you mishandle this milestone, recovery can cost you a lot. For our team, it costs us a potential revenue of 1.5 Million Euros and a huge potential to grow business with FDJ in the future.

Without going into much details, I will list here the lessons one can learn from the above deal.

1. Never price at a round number.

If you give a round number, you are sending a signal that you don't really know what you're doing. Never wonder why supermarkets price an item at 5.99 USD instead of a round 6 USD? On a research by Malia Mason from Columbia Business School, it was demonstrated that:

"Based on social psychology studies, people place more value on precise numbers than on round numbers."

Potential buyers tend to assume that you have done a lot of calculations and

后得出的结果。而将相同的产品定价为 10，000 美元给顾客留下的印象则是：你的定价依据的是含糊或错误的知识，你甚至都没有做足功课来估算出你的产品的真正价值。我们在“一年后见面”和在“365 天后见面”，哪个听起来更可信和明确呢？毫无疑问是后者。

不过也不要走另一个极端，你给出的价格如果太夸张反而可能引起怀疑。9,650 美元的定价就比 9,654.32 美元或者 9,999.99 美元更可信。几美元的差别产生的效果却千差万别。

2. 在宣布一个大项目的最终价格前要先划分你的报价。

将一大块牛排切成一块一块慢慢品尝比一口吞下整块牛排更容易消化。同样，一份 150 万欧元的提案听起来太庞大以至于很难让人消化。如果我们一开始将其划分开来一步步提出，对方可能就会容易接受得多。例如告诉客户在那份 150 万欧元的提案里，包含了两位技术工程师的薪资，他们将会作为“驻场工程师”到客户的公司全职工作 6 个月；还包含一些需要采购的总价值 15 万欧元的硬件，以及设备升级、人员培训、数据管理等一系列的开支。我们在宣布最终价格前没有向该客户划分报价，也没有解释 150 万欧元这个大数字的由来。我们的本意是先提出报价，然后再解释我们出价的细分情况，但是在我们被告知离开时已经无力回天了。**生意场上，意图不重要，行动才重要**。后来回想这段经历时，我站在客户的角度重新审视我们的行为，当时我们就好像在说：“这个项目将花费你 150 万欧元。把钱给我们，剩下的就不用你们操心了。”

3. 在客户那边拥有人脉或朋友并不意味着你的生意有了终身保障。

公司以赚钱为生，而对价格敏感的客户只要他找到更好的选择就会迅速离你而去。无论你接受与否，这都是做生意的冰冷现实。我们的团队谈判时有些乐观过头，因为有高级管理层的推荐，我们便以为会有很高的成交率。

data analysis to reach a price of 9,650 USD. Whereas pricing the same product at 10,000 USD leaves the customer under the impression that you priced based on vague knowledge, or worse, you have not done your homework to estimate the true value of your product. Consider this example: If I tell you "let's meet in 1 year" or "let's meet in 365 days", which one sounds more credible and precise? No doubt the second one.

Do not go to the other extreme by providing a price that sounds too ridiculous or that might raise suspicion. Pricing at 9,650 USD looks more credible than pricing at 9654.32 USD or at 9999.99 USD. A few Dollars difference could make a big difference.

2. Breakdown your quote before you announce the final price of a large project.

A steak sliced into several pieces is easier to digest than a big steak eaten in one bite. A 1.5 Millions proposal sounds too big to digest. It would have made sense if we started off by serving the slices of our offer piece by piece. In the 1.5 Millions proposal, there was incorporated the salary of two technical engineers who would be dispatched as "implants" to sit at the customer's facility full-time for 6 months. There was included some hardware that needed to be acquired for a total sum of 150,000 Euros. There was also the cost of some upgrades, trainings, data management… We didn't break this down to the customer before announcing the final price to explain how we got to the 1.5 Million figure. Our intention was to propose our quote, then explain the details of our offer afterwards. But it was too late when we were told to pack and leave. **In business, intentions don't matter, actions do**. Later on, pondering over this episode, and putting myself in the prospect's shoes, it felt to me as if we said:"The project will cost you 1.5 Millions Euros. Give us your money and trust us with the rest."

3. Just having connections or friends at the customer's side doesn't mean you have business for life.

Companies are in the business of making money and a customer who is price-sensitive will go somewhere else as soon as he finds a better deal. This is the hard reality

这个案例刚好印证了这一点。

4. 一定要在谈判前做好准备。

即使按照市场标准我们的价格是公道且“合理”的，但客户明白这些吗？我们应该在谈判前举行一次内部座谈会，草拟作战计划，详细设计如何提出报价。

回看本书中关于谈判前准备的部分你就会明白，为什么充足的准备能够帮助我们避开问题。

5. 不要畏惧客户。

无论你面前的客户有多强大或者该交易有多重要，都别落入客户的圈套。FDJ 的谈判团队就非常明白这一点。他们打断谈话并要求我们离开的举动便是一种恐吓我们的谈判技巧，并由此占据了谈判上风。这说明他们阴险狡猾吗？不，这只使他们显得无礼。他们在用他们的方式告诉我们“你们的价格太高了，我是不会付那么多的”。很明显，这是一种强势出击的方式。

6. 价值，价值，价值。

你能把潜在客户的注意力从相对较高的价格转移至别处的唯一方式便是将讨论聚焦于价值。况且，**除非你讲出来，否则谁都不知道你的产品有哪些价值**。这些价值能够让客户知道他将得到什么样的潜在利益，或者通过使用你的产品，他可以规避什么样的负面后果。你的价值可以是一支面向客户的高水准团队、基于产品认证的实验测试、多年经验累积起来的强大商业资源、充分优化的配送及供应链系统、优越的付款条件、客户的高度认可、对你某个具体项目加以赞赏的报刊文章等。如果你已成功辨析了客户需求，那么你也应该能够指出在这些需求中哪个因素对客户来说是最重要的。

7. 锁定价格区间。

无论你身处哪个行业，你的价格都最好是固定的，但价格区间可以变化。你可以在保持相同价格的同时减少一些服务。这也是为什么有必要在价

of business whether you accept it or not. Our team was a bit too comfortable walking into the customer's negotiation table, thinking that our chances are high to get the deal because the higher management recommended us. And that leads to the next point.

4. Never go unprepared to a negotiation.

We knew very well that our price was justifiable and "fair" by market standards. But did the customer know? We should have sat down internally before the meeting, and drafted our game plan detailing how to put forward the offer.

Go back to the section of this book where I talk about the preparation for a negotiation, and you will understand why a good preparation could have helped us avoid the disaster.

5. Don't be intimidated by a customer.

No matter how big the customer is or how important the deal is, don't fall in the customer's trap. FDJ's negotiation team knew exactly what they were doing. Asking us to pack our stuff and get out of the room was a negotiation technique to intimidate us and make them gain the upper-hand. Does this make them dishonest? No, it just makes them disrespectful. It was their way of telling us "Your price is too high, and I will not pay that much". An aggressive way obviously.

6. VALUE VALUE VALUE.

The only way you could move the prospect's attention from a price that is relatively high is to shift and refocus the discussion around value. And **no one will know about your value unless you talk about it**. Your value tells the customer what potential beneficial impact he will have, or what negative consequences he will avoid by using your product. Your value could be a highly skilled customer-facing team, lab testing backed by product certifications, strong legacy from years and years of experience in the business, highly optimized delivery and supply chain, favorable payment terms, customers' testimony, press articles praising your handling of a specific project... The list can go on and on. If you have carried the Needs Identification successfully, you should be able to identify which elements of your offering are of the highest importance to the prospect.

格谈判时使用“该产品资费会根据你所需要的功能以及担保类型在 550 到 720 美元之间浮动”这样的说明。由于你并不想让砍价常客每次都知道自己的价格，所以修改价格区间也就比修改固定的价格更加容易。如果你不这么做的话，你只能吸引来那些为寻求最低折扣而在不同供应商之间游走的买家。同时也将拉低你的品牌价值，从长远角度来看，还会损害你的公司形象。

经过 8 周的实习后我离开了那家 IT 公司，后来也没有跟进该公司与那个大客户的业务往来情况。不过在我撰写本书的时候，我特意看了看那家公司的网站，并在网站的“我们的客户”部分看到了 FDJ 的标识，这对他们来说是件好事。

最后，许多销售代表都会在出价阶段使用一些辅助工具，比如说手册或者幻灯片。如果你要这么做，请确保避免以下四种错误：

- ■ 太过专注于演示 PPT 而忽略了潜在客户传递的信号以及肢体语言。
- ■ 用长达 2 小时的 PPT 演讲挑战听众的耐心，特别是在某个复杂的销售情境下。

相反，将你的演讲分为 3 或 4 个部分。在每个部分结束的时候，暂停并询问“你们觉得这些信息足够让你们做出决定了吗”，如果回答是否定的，那就继续。这个问题其实很有分量，因为这也能够让你明白自己的谈话对象是否为真正的决策者。

- ■ 内容使人迷惑而不是令人信服。

你的 PPT 内容或许在你看来是合乎逻辑的，但对潜在客户来说可能毫无头绪。试着向你的同事或经理展示你的 PPT，从而了解你的内容在他人眼中所呈现的样子。

7. Tie the scope to the price.

No matter what line of business you are in, the price might be fixed and not negotiable, but the scope never is. You can keep the same price but take away pieces of the offering. That's why it is always helpful to start the price negotiation with "This product costs between 550 USD and 720 USD depending on the features you'd like to add to it, and the type of guarantee we will be looking into". It is easier to modify the scope instead of the price because you don't want to be known as the company that cuts its prices every time it faces an objection. If you do not do that, you will only attract the type of buyers who move from one supplier to another looking only for the deepest discount. You will also cheapen the value of your brand and alter the image of your company on the long run.

I left the small IT company after my eight-week internship, and didn't follow-up at that time to find out how the relationship developed with that specific customer. But while writing this book, I went back to that company's website, and under the "Our Clients" section, I found the FDJ logo. Good for them.

Finally, many sales representatives use some kind of support during the Offer Making phase, such as a brochure or PowerPoint slides. If you do so, make sure to avoid these 4 mistakes:

- Getting too absorbed by the presentation to the point where you ignore the prospect's signals and body-language.
- Annoying your audience with 2 hours PowerPoint presentations, especially when you are making a complex sale.

Instead, break your presentation into 3 or 4 parts. At the end of each part, pause and ask "Have you seen enough information to make a decision?" If the answer is no, then proceed. That question is very powerful because it will also allow you to sense if you are talking to the right decision makers.

- Confusing instead of convincing.

■ 没有潜在客户参与的单向演讲。

即使是用手册或者 PPT，你也应该通过提问和引导互动的方式来鼓动潜在客户参与。在这个过程中你将遇到客户购买阻力。

阶段 3：应对客户购买阻力

客户："我今天什么都不会买。"

销售员："先生，如果您今天什么都不买不是您的问题，是我的失误！"

潜在客户购买阻力的出现才是一场谈判真正的开始。当一名销售代表向潜在客户谈及自己所提供服务的好处或向对方演示其产品的功能时，该潜在买家可能会提出声明或问题以表现不愿购买的意向。这些便是购买阻力。无论你多么擅长销售，都会在销售谈判的过程中面临潜在客户的某种抵触。如果不存在销售阻力，那也就不需要销售人员了，生活中的所有事物就会像超市里的商品，买家走进去，挑选好想要的，付款，然后离开。

1. 为什么会有购买阻力呢？

有以下几个原因：

■ 这是潜在客户策略的一部分，买家会故意降低你产品的价值，压制你以获得更好的价格。

■ 这是潜在客户心理状态和预设的一部分，他们只要一见到销售代表就会想着抵抗。

■ 该潜在客户或许没有购买权限，因此通过设限和抵制的方式加以掩饰。许多公司都需要获得他们海外母公司的授权后才能继续购买行为。

The content of your PowerPoint might look logical to you, but makes no sense to the prospect. Try to show your slides to a colleague or a manager to see how your content is perceived by other people.

- Making it a one-way presentation where you do the talk and the prospect is sitting there listening.

Even with a brochure or slides presentation, you should be able to engage the prospect by asking questions and provoking interactions. That's how you will start hearing some of the customer's objections.

Phase 3: Objections handling

Customer: "I'm not buying anything today."

Salesman: "Sir, if you don't buy anything today it will be my fault, not yours!"

Serious negotiations don't begin until the prospect's objections surface. When a sales representative talks to a prospect about the benefits of using his service, or demonstrates a feature of his product, the potential buyer might put forward statements or ask questions indicating unwillingness to buy. These are called objections. No matter how good you are at sales, you will get some resistance from the prospect during the sales negotiation process. If there were no sales resistances, there wouldn't be a need for salespeople... Everything in life would be like a supermarket where the buyer walks in, picks what he wants, pays, and walks out.

1. So, why do objections arise?

They arise because either:

- They are part of the prospect's strategy. The buyer will try to lower the value of your product to squeeze you for better prices.
- They are part of the prospect's mental conditioning and programming. As soon as they see a sales representative they think about resistance.

如果潜在客户提出了购买阻力，试着仔细聆听并从中提取出额外的信息，从而进一步理解他的顾虑。**购买阻力并不意味着“不”，而仅仅意味着“暂时还没有”**。在现实中你很少会遇到足够诚实的潜在客户，直接告诉你“好的，我喜欢你的服务，我只是还不太相信你。”

先不说购买阻力是否合理，在探讨那些你可以用来回应购买阻力的技巧之前，我们先来谈谈成功应对购买阻力的五项守则。

2. 应对购买阻力的五项守则。

守则 1：感恩。

与潜在客户有良性的互动是件好事，特别是当**购买阻力成为潜在客户想要告诉你如何向他们推销的一种潜意识时**。最糟糕的潜在客户是那种坐在桌子对面一直听着你讲，一旦你展示完产品及服务，就让你留下一份宣传手册并告诉你如果他们感兴趣的话会联系你的人。

守则 2：避免与买家争论。

赢得争论并不意味着赢得销售。在谈判过程中应当先将情绪放到一边，因为潜在客户在批判你的产品时并不意味着是在批判你。当你被自己的情绪主导时，你的判断就会受到影响，这样你便会丧失本应具备的客观性来评判当时的情境。你甚至会发火而说出一些后悔莫及的话。

守则 3：永远不要伪造答案。

如果潜在客户提出的购买阻力是你无法回答或难以置评的，那说句“抱歉，这一点我不是非常确定，请允许我请示完领导再给您回复”也无妨。这一点不仅在谈判的这一阶段有效，在交易的任何阶段都是行得通的。

守则 4：保持乐观和自信。

处理购买阻力有时会很困难，特别是在你销售的产品或服务耗费了大量资金和时间的情况下。潜在客户仅仅一句“你的产品太落后了，有比你们先

■ The prospect may lack the authority to buy, and he covers it by putting limitations and showing resistances. Many companies would need authorization from their overseas parent company to proceed with the purchase.

If the prospect puts forward an objection, try to listen carefully and extract additional information from him to better understand his concern. **Objections don't always mean "No", they just mean "Not yet"**.The fact is that you will rarely come across a prospect who is honest enough to tell you "Well, I like your service, but I just don't trust you yet."

Regardless of the objection being valid or not, and before we discuss the techniques you can use to respond to objections, let's talk about the 5 rules of successful objection handling.

2.Handling the buyer's objections — Five rules.

Rule 1: Be grateful.

Having a healthy exchange with a prospect is always a good thing, especially when the **objections become the prospect's subconscious telling you how to sell to them**. The worst prospect is the one who sits across the table, listens to you all the way, and once you're done presenting your product/service, asks you to leave your brochure and expect a call if they are interested.

Rule 2: Avoid getting into an argument with the buyer.

You don't win sales by winning arguments. Emotions should be left aside during the negotiation process because a prospect who criticizes your product is not necessarily criticizing you. When your emotions take over, your judgment is affected and you lose the objectivity needed to evaluate situations. You might even lose temper and say things you will regret later on.

Rule 3: Never fake an answer.

If the prospect raises an objection to which you don't have an answer or on which you can't comment, there is no harm in saying "Sorry, I am not sure about this point, but let me check with my management and let you know". This is not

进很多的公司也在联系我们”或者“我听说从上个月开始你们的产品由于点火装置开关的缺陷问题而不得不全部召回”就可能伤害你的自尊。不论这些言论是否属实，你都要保持镇定自若。在从容回应的同时不要显示出任何气愤或者沮丧的情绪。因为当你回到自己的办公室后有很多时间可以用来抚慰自己。

守则 5：及时处理购买阻力。

你面临的任何购买阻力都需要立刻处理。如果你没有在会谈过程中对其进行处理，这个问题在你离开后也不会消失。如果你当时无法马上解决，那就明确地告诉客户你会在后续的谈话或者电话回访中解决该问题。**就我个人而言，我从没因为无视一个问题而使其不再出现**。它明天依然存在，除非你去解决它，否则它会一直恶化下去。就像你早上没有洗碗就离开家，晚上回到家的时候期待碗筷都已经自己洗干净一样，不会的！事情只会随着时间的流逝越来越混乱。

3. 合理的购买阻力。

当然，并非所有的购买阻力都是不恰当的。当它们与以下几点相关时就是完全合理的：

■ 具体的担忧

潜在客户提出“你的价格比其他人高很多”。

■ 看法或成见

潜在客户提出“使用这种化学物质不安全”。

■ 优先级

潜在客户提出“这不是我们今年优先考虑的事项”。

■ 缺乏认知

valid only in this phase of the negotiation. It is valid for any exchange that takes place with the other party.

Rule 4 : Be positive and confident.

Objections can sometimes be hard to take, especially when you are selling a product or service on which you spent much money and much time. It could take the prospect a few words to shutter your pride simply by saying "Your product is way behind. We are getting offers on products that are a lot more advanced." or "I heard that you had to recall all your products from last month because of an ignition switch defect". Whether these statements are true or false, stay calm and composed. Answer with confidence and don't show any emotions by displaying anger or grief. You have plenty of time to lick your wounds in privacy once you return to your office.

Rule 5 : Address the objections.

Any objection you hear needs to be addressed right away. If it is not addressed during the meeting, it will come back and hunt you after you leave. If you can't address an objection right there and then, make it clear to the customer that you will either put it aside until you come back to it later during the talk, or will follow up with a call to address it after you leave. **I have personally never run across a problem that went away because we ignored it**. It will be there tomorrow, and it will keep getting worse until it's resolved. It's like leaving your home in the morning without cleaning the dishes, and coming back home in the evening hoping that the dishes would have cleaned themselves. No! Things will only get messier as time passes by.

3.Some objections are reasonable.

Needless to say, not all objections are irrelevant. They can be completely legitimate when they are related to the following points:

■ Specific concern.

Prospect's objection: "Your price is a lot higher than everybody else's."

■ Perception.

Prospect's objection: "The use of this chemical is not safe."

潜在客户提出“我们不需要责任保险”。

为确保你不在阻力应对阶段错过任何信息，请记住要不时地向潜在客户询问并获得澄清。比如你可以简单地说：“您介意在这个方面做些更深入的解释吗？”

如果你发觉对方不再提问，那便是时候深入推进了。

如果你已经恰当地回应了潜在客户的所有问题，是不是就可以成交了？不一定。这时候往往会有些隐藏的购买阻力需要你在它们浮出水面之前进行发掘。当我认为自己已经发现并处理了潜在客户提出的所有问题时，我还会再加一句“到目前为止，您还有其他我没有解答的问题或者担忧吗”或“看来您对这个项目的推进方式有很多的忧虑，您还有哪些问题”。

4. 10 个回应购买阻力的技巧。

以上的这些守则和提示都取决于你的**态度**。它们并没有告诉你面对购买阻力要具体阐述哪些内容，仅仅回答了“当潜在客户提出购买阻力时我应该做出什么反应”这样的问题。现在我们就来看看几条能够让你用令人信服的回答回应购买阻力的技巧。技巧数以百计，为避免冗长，我们精选出 10 条予以讲解。

技巧 1：问术。

这个技巧就是将潜在客户的问题转化为一个提问，并将客户的注意力转移至你的某方面或多个方面的优势上去。

举例：

潜在客户：“你的服务费比市场上的一般标准贵 8%。”

卖家：“是的，不过从长远来看，更好的品质意味着更低的服务费用，您同意我这个观点吗？”

技巧 2：直接否定。

当潜在客户对你公司的产品和服务发表了错误的观点时你便可以运用这

■ Prioritization.

Prospect's objection: "That's not a priority for us this year."

■ Lack of knowledge.

Prospect's objection: "We don't need liability insurance."

To make sure you don't miss anything during the Objections Handling phase, remember to ask the prospect for clarifications every once and then. A quick way would be to say "Would you mind explaining this aspect a bit further?"

If you get to the point where you think that the other party has no objections to voice, it's time to dig further.

If you have answered all the prospect's objections properly, you should be able to close the deal, right? Not necessarily. More often than not, there are hidden objections that will need some digging before they come out. When I feel that I uncovered and addressed all the objections that the prospect might have, I almost always add"Do you have any questions or concerns that I haven't covered so far?"or"It sounds like you have a lot of concerns regarding the way this project is going. What else is in your mind?"

4.Ten techniques to answer the buyer's resistances.

The above rules and guidelines are all about your **attitude**. They don't tell you what to respond to an objection, they just answer the question "How should I react when the prospect hits me with an objection". Now let's look at a few techniques that will help you respond to objections with convincing answers. There are literally hundreds of techniques but we will limit ourselves to just 10 of them in this book to avoid redundancy.

Technique 1: Questioning.

This technique consists of turning the prospect's objection into a question and refocusing on one or many of your strengths.

Example:

Prospect: "Your service is 8% more expensive than the market standard."

个技巧，不过也别太过冒犯或者无礼。

举例：

潜在客户："我从同事那儿听说你们的经理因为诈骗被调查了。"

卖家："我不确定您是从哪里听到的这个消息，我们没有任何一位经理因为诈骗或者其他违法行为而被调查过。正直是我们公司的三大核心价值观之一。"

技巧 3：间接否定。

相比直接否定，这种方式更加委婉。它就是先接受潜在客户的言论，再向其解释为什么他们的观点是错的。

举例：

潜在客户："你们同时为这么多客户提供服务，我不确定是否还能很好地服务我们。"

卖家："确实有很多公司都很信任我们。我们的客户满意率也在去年达到了 95%，并保持逐年上升的势头。"

技巧 4：弱项修正。

这个方法就是将潜在客户的注意力从你产品的弱项转移至强项上。

举例：

潜在客户："你们的机器太慢了。目前我们的机器速率比你们的快两倍。"

卖家："我们的机器确实比你们的慢了一半，但是它也节省了 50% 的费用且退货率降低了 20%。"

技巧 5：共情—类比—验证。

这是我最喜欢用的技巧。这个方法就是通过认清潜在客户的感受，引入多方类似案例，然后用合乎情理的论据进行反击。

举例：

潜在客户："我觉得你们的产品太贵了，而且贵得毫无道理。"

Seller: "Yes, it is slightly more expensive, but do you agree with me that better quality means lower service costs for you in the long term? "

Technique 2: Direct Denial.

This is used when the prospect states a false statement about your company of your products and services. Don't get too defensive or insulting here.

Example:

Prospect: "I heard from a colleague that your managers were investigated for fraud. "

Seller:"I'm not sure where you could have heard that. None of our managers has ever been investigated for a fraud or any other unlawful practice. Integrity is one of our company's 3 core values."

Technique 3: Indirect Denial.

Less threatening than the Direct Denial technique, this one consists of agreeing with the prospect, and then explaining why their statement is wrong.

Example:

Prospect: "Your customer service deals with so many customers at the same time. I'm not sure whether they can accommodate one more customer like me."

Seller: "It is true that many companies have trusted us with their business. Our customer satisfaction has reached 95% last year and it keeps improving year over year. "

Technique 4: Compensating for Deficiencies.

It consists of moving the prospect's attention from a feature your product performs poorly to one in which it excels.

Example:

Prospect: "The output of your machine is too slow. Our current one's output is two times faster."

Seller: "I agree with you that our machine is two times slower, but it also costs 50% less and has 20% less returns."

Technique 5: Feel-Felt-Found.

This one is my favorite. It consists of acknowledging the prospect's feelings, extending them to a larger audience, then firing back with a legitimate argument.

卖家："是的，我们的产品价格是有些高，我也理解您为什么会有这样的感受（共情）。其他客户刚开始使用我们产品的时候也会有相同的感受（类比）。不过当他们接触并享受到我们产品更高的品质后，他们便明白了这样的投资物有所值（验证）。"

技巧6：第三方宣传。

事实总会使你的回答更加有力。如果你的服务让某位客户的生活变得更好了，那就毫不犹豫地拿他们作为增加自己可信度的案例吧。

举例：

潜在客户："我几年前曾与你们有过商业合作，但是后来因为你们糟糕的技术支持而停止合作了。"

卖家："我们过去在技术支持上确实面临一些挑战，不过我们已经对相关部门进行了重组并在两年前聘请了一名经理。目前技术方面的运转情况非常不错。客户X之前也和你们有相同的感受，不过他还是决定尝试与我们合作。现在他对我们的水准和服务非常满意。"

技巧7："强势反击"。

这个方法相对强势，但是对于那些以"需要更多时间来做决定"为借口的购买阻力非常有效。它将客户的某种担忧转化为一个行动的理由。

举例：

潜在客户："我已经对你的产品有足够的了解了，我需要些时间来想想你的提案。"

卖家："我理解这对您的公司来说是个重要的决定，但是延缓您的订单只会增加您公司的花费。我们的产品将为您节省近30%的开销，因此您越早使用我们公司的产品或服务，就能越早节省开支。"

如果你不太愿意使用这种方法，那就试试别的，千万别让谈话就此打住。

Example:

Prospect:"I think your products are too expensive and nothing justifies the higher price."

Seller: "Yes, our prices are slightly higher and I understand why you feel this way. Other customers felt the same way when they started using our product. But once they used it and enjoyed its higher quality, they found that it is worth the investment. "

Technique 6: Third-party Endorsements.

Hard facts will always make your response stronger. If your services have made someone else's life better, don't hesitate to use them as an example to add credibility.

Example:

Prospect: "I did business with you a few years ago but stopped dealing with you because your tech support was so bad."

Seller: "I agree that our tech support has faced a few challenges in the past, but we have restructured the department and brought onboard a new manager 2 years ago. Things are going perfectly well. Customer X felt the same way but decided to try us anyways. Now he is extremely satisfied with our level or service."

Technique 7: "Bouncing-back".

This technique is relatively aggressive but works well with objections about "needing more time to decide". It consists of turning a customer's concern into a reason for action.

Example:

Prospect: "I believe now I have all the details I need regarding your product. I will need some time to think about your proposal."

Seller: "I understand this is an important decision for your company. But delaying your order will only cost your company more money. My product will save you nearly 30%, so the sooner you start using it the better it will be for your savings. "

If you don't feel too comfortable using the Bounce-Back technique, try another approach. Don't end the discussion there. Ask what parts of the proposal the

问问潜在客户需要对提案的哪一个部分再作考虑，这样一来原本即将结束的谈话就可以重新开始。

另一种谈论这种借口的方式是：“大多数看了我的报价之后需要更多时间考虑的人们其实是想了解三个要素之一：我、商品、价格。请问您想要了解哪一个？”

技巧 8：拖延。

这个技巧可以用来将某个话题拖延至谈话的后续阶段。当客户在谈判刚开始，甚至在你还没有展示提案的价值所在前就询问价格时，这个方法非常有用。

举例：

潜在客户：“你的产品多少钱？”

卖家：“在回答这个问题之前，我希望您可以给我几分钟的时间来了解贵公司有什么样的具体需求，然后我再根据这些需求给出相应的价格提案。”

万一该潜在客户执意要知道价格，那你也不要给出一个确切的最终价格。最好给客户一个价格区间，以便你根据交易的实际情况来提高或降低价格。比如你可以这么说：“根据您的具体需求，某一相似的产品的费用是 1,000~1,500 美元，让我多问您几个问题，以便更好地了解您的确切需求，给您更准确的报价。”

技巧 9：试用。

这个方法仅适用于部分产品或服务，但却是你不用多说就能展现价值的最好方式。即在潜在客户确定下单前，允许他们免费使用你的产品或服务一段时间。

举例：

潜在客户：“我不太想在今天就承诺买你们公司的复印机，你们的机器看起来复杂又难用。”

卖家：“我理解。要不我让客户服务部先在您的办公室安装一台复印机并让您免费体验 10 天，我会在 10 天后来听取您的反馈，您觉得如何？”

prospect will need to think more about. That could re-start a conversation that was about to end.

Another way to talk this excuse would be to say: “Most people who ask for more time to review my proposal say so because they want more time to think about one of the 3 M’s: Me, Merchandise, Money. Which one of those three you’d like to think over.”

Technique 8: Deferring.

It is used to push a topic to later stages of the discussion. It is very useful when the customer asks about your price at the very beginning of the negotiation, before you even demonstrate the value of your offering.

Example:

Prospect: “How much is your product? ”

Seller: “I would ask you to hold off for a few minutes in order for me to identify what specs will exactly match your needs, then I can make a final proposal. ”

In case the prospect insists on knowing the price, do not give a firm and final price. Better give a bracket that will allow you to push the price up or down depending on the scope of the transaction. A way to put it is “A similar product will cost you anything between 1,000 USD and 1,500 USD depending on the specifications you need. Let me ask you a couple of more questions to understand your exact needs so I can give you an exact price”.

Technique 9: Trial Offer.

This only applies in the case of some products or services, but it is the best way to demonstrate your value without much talk. It consists of letting the prospect use your product or service for some time for free before they commit to a firm order.

Example:

Prospect: “I’m not willing to make a commitment to buy your copy machine today. It looks complex and hard to use.”

Seller: “I understand. How about I ask our service department to install one in your office for 10 days for free today, and I will come back in 10 days to see if it was

你在用这个技巧的时候，请记住要明确租借条款的内容，以防你在后续回访时太过“惊喜”。

技巧 10：明确成交。

如果他们同意成交，销售代表愿意为潜在客户解决相应的购买阻力。请记住在这种情况下一定要加上一个时间期限。

举例：

销售代表：“如果我现在就能为您展示这个型号的机器并不比更小的机器难用的话，您愿意和我们合作吗？”

我相信你从以上 10 条技巧可以看到一些倾向，它们不仅可以单独运用也能综合使用。

现在就看你如何把它们融入你的具体情境中去了。积极主动的销售代表在阅读本书时应该会马上拿出笔记本和笔，列出自己在实战中经常遇到的购买阻力，然后再逐个给出可供使用的回应方式和答复内容。

5. 如何回应“你的价格太高了”。

really that hard to use."

If you use this technique, remember to clearly define the terms of the lease so you don't have any surprises when you show up later.

Technique 10: Certain Closure.

Here the sales representative would offer to resolve the prospect's objection if they make the purchase. Remember to always add a time constraint to the equation.

Example:

Sales representative: "If I could show you right now that using a machine of this size is no more difficult than using smaller machines, can we do business?"

I believe you could see the trend from the above 10 techniques. They can work separately or combinedly.

Now it's up to you to adapt them to fit your specific context. A proactive sales representative who is reading this book would right now grab a pen and a notebook, and list on one column all the objections he often hears in the field, then list on the column next to it all the responses he could use to fire back.

5.Dealing with the "Your price is too high" objection.

在与来自世界各地的销售人员进行上百次讨论后，我听到了一个共同的购买阻力，那就是“你的价格太高了”。所以我会在这个特定的购买阻力上多花些时间，来解释某个潜在客户向你提出这个问题时该如何回应。你可能会从潜在客户那儿听到以下版本：

- 这个太贵了。
- 我能在 XYZ 商店获得更便宜的价格。
- 如果你想要合作就必须重新考虑你的价格。
- 我们无法为这个产品 / 服务支付那么多钱。

它们的意思都一样——你的价格太高了。客户只是试着用谎言来寻求更好的价格？还是说他是认真的？

如果你的潜在客户告诉你你的产品价格太高了，你其实应该心怀感激。你应该知道，很多买家根本不会给你任何反馈，而是直接走开。另一个你应该心怀感激的理由是如今的一些老练的买家只会告诉你他们需要什么、何时需要、需要的程度如何，以及会为此支付多少，然后告诉你“要么接受，要么放弃”。我曾合作的通用电气的一家公司分部在 2009 年采购供应链服务时便是这么做的。该公司将各物流公司的代表邀请到他们的一个大会议室。进去之前，每个物流公司都会拿到一个按钮。在某个特定的时间，该公司采购团队走进来，开始逐页地放 PPT。一张张幻灯片分别罗列着他们所期待的服务、时间表、细节以及他们会为此支付的价格。如果你的物流公司对幻灯片页面上的价格和条款没有异议，那就按下按钮。如果不同意，那就继续等待下一张幻灯片。这就是该公司用他们的方式说：“这是我们需要的内容，这是我们需要的方式，这是我们愿意付的价格。要么接受，要么放弃。”

那么，你该如何回应“你的价格太高了”呢？

From the hundreds of discussions that I had with salespeople from around the world, there was one objection that I heard from every audience I interacted with. And that objection is "Your price is too high." So I will spend a bit more time on this specific objection and explain how you could respond if a potential buyer puts it forward. Other versions you have probably heard from your prospect:

- This is very expensive.
- I can get it cheaper at XYZ shop.
- You must review your prices if you want this business.
- We can not pay that much for this product/service.

They all mean the same thing: "Your price is too high". What if your customer is lying to try and get a better deal? But what if he is not?

If your potential customer tells you that your price is too high, you should be grateful. As you already probably know, many buyers don't give any feed-back.They just walk away. Another reason to be grateful is that today's sophisticated buyers tell you what they need, when they need it, how they need it, and how much they will pay for it, then you are told to "take it or leave it". That's how one of the General Electric divisions I have worked with in 2009 used to buy its supply chain services. General Electric (GE) Healthcare would invite representatives of logistics companies to a big room at their office. Each logistics company was handed a button and asked to proceed to the meeting room. At the specified time, GE buying team would walk in, put up a PowerPoint and start moving from one slide to the next. Every slide had the service they expected, the timelines, the details, and the price they will pay for it. If your logistics company agrees to the price and the terms on the slide, it should hit the button. If it does not, it should sit there and wait for the next slide. This was GE's way of saying: "Here is what we need, here is how we need it, and here is how much we will pay for it. Take it or leave it."

策略 1：不给买家说这句话的机会。

一种直截了当的方式便是在你被问及价格前询问“您有多少预算给这个项目”。在谈判早期阶段，你可以用一个价格区间来测试他们的反应，如这个型号的价格是 2.5 万 ~ 3 万美元，这么做可以让你有足够的价格调整空间以证明你对这笔交易的诚意。

策略 2：挑战他们。

“你的价格太高了”是一个主观的表述。这让我想起了另一个主观表述，一个我几乎每天都会从客户那儿听到的话：“这件事非常紧急。”每当我听到这样的话，我就会反问：“有多紧急？你们确切的截止日期是哪天？”如果一个人需要做一台手术，那么其紧急程度可以用“小时”来表示，如果一个人需要协商一份长达 30 多页的法律合同，其紧急程度可以用“天”来表示，这是主观性的。

在涉及价格的时候，问一句“我们的价格高了多少？”或者“我的价格到底有多高？”而事实是无论你做什么生意，你的价格总会比其他某个人的要高。就算你销售的产品价格为 10 万美元，而你的竞争者卖 9.95 万美元，你的价格依旧更高。

这一点无须多言，一名训练有素的销售代表永远都知道他的竞争者的价格以及折扣策略。

策略 3：赞同并将谈话从价格转移至价值。

这时你已经不再是防守方了，谈判应该变成一个交互式的讨论，你要确认客户的预期以及对客户来说什么是最有价值的收益，并相应地给出一个提案。大多成功的谈判都来自出色的价值论证。我在开始一场销售谈判前都会在心里重复这样一句话**“我来的目的不是将利润最大化，而是将机会最大化”**。当然，并不是说将利润最大化会伤害到谁，所有做生意的人都是为了利润最大化。不过如果你用另一个视角来看，你越是将机会最大化，你就会有越多

So, how should you respond to "Your price is too high"?

Strategy 1: Don't even let the buyer get there.

A straight forward way would be to ask "What budget are you allocating to this project?" before you are asked for your prices. At early stages, a price bracket could be put forward to gauge their reaction: "For an order of this size, you are looking at something around 25,000 USD ~30,000 USD". This will allow you to have enough movement on the price to demonstrate that you want this deal to materialize.

Strategy 2: Challenge them.

"Your price is too high" is a subjective statement. It reminds me of an equally subjective statement that I hear almost every day from customers: "This is really urgent". When I hear that, I simply replicate "How urgent is it? What is your exact deadline?"If someone needs to undergo a surgery, then urgency is a matter of"hours". If someone needs to negotiate a 30-page legal contract, then the urgency is a matter of "days". It is subjective.

In the case of pricing, ask "How much too high are we?" or "How high is my price exactly?" The fact is that your price will always be higher than someone else's, no matter what you do. If you are selling a product for 100,000 USD and your competitor is selling it for 99,500 USD, then your price is still higher.

Needless to say, an educated sales representative always knows the competition's prices and discount strategies.

Strategy 3: Agree and shift the discussion from price to value.

You are not on the defensive anymore. This should be an interactive discussion where you are validating expectations and understanding what benefits are of most value to your buyer, then making an offer that is consistent with that. Most successful negotiations are a result of good value demonstration. Before I walk into a sales negotiation, I repeat a few times in my head "**I am not here to maximize profit. I am here to maximize opportunity**". Of course maximizing profit doesn't hurt anyone. Everybody is in business to maximize profit. But when you look at it from

的潜在盈利机会。最大化机会意味着，我不是来和潜在客户分一张“饼”的，而是来和他共同探讨怎样通过商议解决方案和论证价值来“画大”这块饼的。一旦你有了这样的思维，你就会发现自己可以一直产生新的想法，拓展新的机会空间。

策略 4：重新评估你的价格。

评估定价并将其与未来交易承诺联系起来。即使这个评估会令对方不愉快，也有必要提出来，否则你将会失去让步的机会并因此在谈判桌上错失潜在的收入。

在承诺重新审视价格前请求对方给你一些时间，用以在内部商议价格。来看这个例子：

买家：“这个多少钱？”

卖家：“185 美元。”

买家：“这个价格太高了。”

卖家：“好吧，给我 150 美元我们就成交。”

在这个交易中买家会怎么想？他绝对会觉得卖家在对他敲竹杠。他要么会要求一个更低的价格，要么会用一两个无关紧要的问题打发你走人。知道如何表述降价和降价本身一样重要。

策略 5：在你不得已要离开的时候，不要害怕。

这是最后一个策略，也是你可以使用的最后一招。其实有时买家心里早就有选好的合作伙伴，他只是想把你当作一个知识和情报的来源而已。有些时候“你的价格太高了”仅仅是个噱头。请记得要保持敬意地告诉他们：“这样看来我们可能并非是您的最佳选择。我希望您不会因为我们不愿降低价格而感到不快。”不妨要求将该客户关联到你公司的电子邮件推送列表中。

a different perspective, the more you maximize opportunities, the more potential you create for your profit to grow. Opportunity maximization means I am not sitting down with the prospect to slice up and divide a "pie". I am rather discussing how to "grow" that pie together by proposing solutions and demonstrating value. As soon as your brain is conditioned in that way, you will notice that you are forcing yourself to always propose new ideas and expand a scope.

Strategy 4: Review your pricing.

But tie it to a commitment to future business. Even if that commitment is not honored by the other party, it still is important to ask for it, otherwise you will be handing out concessions freely, hence leaving potential money on the table.

Ask for some time to review the pricing internally before committing to a price review. Consider this exchange:

Buyer: "How much is this? "
Seller: "185 USD."
Buyer: "The price is too high."
Seller: "OK, give me 150 USD and it's yours. "

How would the buyer feel about this exchange? He certainly feels that the seller tried to rip him off. He will either ask for an even lower price, or ask one or two random questions before walking out with no purchase. Knowing how to announce a lower price is as important as the price reduction itself.

Strategy 5: Move on. Don't be afraid to walk away when you have to.

This is the last strategy because it should be your last resort solution. Sometimes the buyer has already pre-selected a friend to whom he intends to award the business, but he just wants to use you as a source of knowledge and intelligence. Some other times the "Your price is too high" is a bluff. Remember to stay respectful: "In this situation, we may not be the best solution for you. I hope you won't be upset if we decline to make a lower offer." It doesn't hurt to try and hook the customer up to your company, by asking, for example, to sign them up to your email marketing list.

在进入本书的下一章之前，还有 3 个销售人员的重要实践需要介绍。

实践 1：在客户提出异议之前自己主动提出来。举个例子，如果你的价格太高了，并且你每次跟潜在客户提起的时候，你都会听到这个异议，那么，你在报价时可以用这种方式：“先生，我从我的很多客户那里收到了我们的价格比我们的竞争对手要高的反馈，这是事实。我们的价格确实比他们稍微高一点，然而，我们提供了一些他们没有的服务，让我给您展示下……”

实践 2：当客户讲出一个顾虑的时候，询问客户：“这是唯一一个阻止您继续这个谈判的因素吗？”有一些潜在客户将会告诉你你的价格太高，而当你解决了这个顾虑让他们签单的时候，他们又会告诉你你们发货太慢。当你搞定了一个顾虑之后，他们又会提出另一个。因此，你最好能确认他们提到的顾虑是唯一的一个顾虑，一旦你解决了这个顾虑，你基本上就可以成功拿下这单了。

实践 3：有时候，潜在客户事先已经知道了你的价格，并且在了解你们产品真正的价值前先提到了对价格的异议。如果是这种情况，你需要争取更多的时间来谈论产品的价值以及你的产品或者服务是如何完美地满足他们的需求的。如果潜在客户一上来就质疑价格太高，我会说：“如果我可以向您展示我的报价可以组合成各种形式来满足您任何的预算的话，我们可以继续往下谈吗？”一旦他们说了是，而且他们通常都会说是，我会继续我的价值展示。

Before moving on to the next section of the book, there are three important practices that are common among salespeople that are worth mentioning.

Practice 1: It consists of bringing up objections before they emerge. In other words, talking about those objections yourself before the prospect does. For instance, if your price is too high, and you know that you always hear this objection every time you talk to a prospect, then you can mention your high price during the Offer Making phase in these terms: "Mr. customer, we hear from most of our clients that our price is higher than our competitors' price. That is true. Our price is slightly higher than theirs, however, we offer something that they don't. Let me show you how this feature is…"

Practice 2: It consists of asking the customer "Is this the only thing preventing you from going ahead with this deal?" when the customer brings up an objection. The reason is that some prospects will tell you that your price is too high, and once you address this objection and you ask them to close, they will tell you that your delivery is too slow. Once you tackle this objection, they will move on to the next one. Hence, it is better to make sure that the objection they raised is the only one they have, and once you tackle it you can attempt to close the deal.

Practice 3: Sometimes the prospect already knows your price, and brings up the price objection before he understands the true value of your offering. In that case, you want to buy some more time to talk about your value and how your product or service perfectly fits in perfectly. When the prospect claims early on that my price is too high, I would say "If I can show you that our offer could be packaged in a way that can fit any budget, would that be a good step forward?" Once they say yes, and they often do, I carry on with my value demonstration.

成交

虽然你知道如何主导一次出色的销售谈判，但是每次在谈判的最后阶段你想要完成交易的时候都会感到不自然。即使你知道该潜在客户已经完全折服并准备购买了，你还是很难找到一种既不过分内敛，又不过于强势的方式来结束谈判。那该怎么继续呢？

市场营销人员负责将马带到水源，销售人员则负责让马喝水。也就是说，销售人员的职责是激起一个反应，而这个反应就是让潜在客户说“成交”。成交是销售流程中最敏感的一步。既然如此，你该如何激起这个反应呢？

提示 1: 成为一名销售顾问

首先，作为一名销售代表，你应该将自己从眼前的需求转移到尽快完成

Closing the deal

You know how to lead a good sales negotiation, but you feel like you stumble every time you want to close a deal at the late stages of the negotiation. Even when you know that the prospect is completely sold and ready to buy, you find it hard to adopt a balanced approach that is not too shy, yet not too aggressive. How to proceed?

Marketing people bring the horse to the water. Salespeople make the horse drink. That is to say, sales' role is to provoke a reaction, and that ultimate reaction should be for the prospect to say "We have a deal". Closing is the most sensitive step in the sales process. So, how do you provoke that reaction?

Pointer 1: Be a Sales Consultant

First and foremost, as a sales representative, you should remove yourself from

交易中去，并让潜在客户将你视为一名销售顾问。你应该先花点时间把我们在本书中探讨过的步骤进行回顾，逐条去做的同时要与潜在客户分享对他们有帮助的深刻见解。这类信息是超越表象的。人们通常更加倾向于和能够给他们提供有深刻见解的信息并帮助他们做出明智抉择的销售代表签下合同。我的朋友克劳德是一家美国财富 500 强公司驻迪拜的销售经理。我有一次问他为什么在销售上如此成功，他答道:“学识，学识赢得尊重。我的潜在客户都认为我是一个学识渊博的人。在 21 世纪，你很少会碰上一个无知的客户，因为任何人花上几分钟时间在网上搜索一下就可以告诉你一个产品或服务应该值多少钱。我确信我与客户分享了不少资讯和知识，所以他们才会敞开心扉，并最终与我成交。也就是说我会在参加会议前做好充分的准备，因为信息分享的过程也是我向客户展现提案附加值的过程。”这段话告诉我们：我们要做的是被客户视为一名“顾问”，而非一个普通的“销售代表”。

提示 2: 成交前的话术

那么，在你处理好潜在客户所有的购买阻力并察觉到他已经准备好向前推进后，你该做什么呢？是说“感谢您的到来，非常高兴能与您对话，保持联系，再见”？还是手指交叉地坐在那儿，等着客户告诉你“好的，我准备好成交了，是现在吗”？都不是。请记住你为什么来这儿：成交。与潜在客户有一个愉快的谈判是好事，但是销售人员的佣金不是依据谈判的愉快程度而定的，而是依据成交的数量。如果你已经评估过需求，报过价并处理好了潜在客户所有的购买阻力，那就可以完成交易了。就是这么简单。根据与你谈判的潜在客户的个性，你可以直接或者间接地说出来。

the short term need to close the deal as quickly as possible, and let the prospect start perceiving you as a sales consultant. You should take the time to first go through all the steps we have discussed previously in this book, and do that while sharing with the prospect useful insight that will help them in their business. Insight means information beyond the obvious. People are more likely to sign a deal with the sales representative that provides useful insight for them and helps them make educated choices. My friend Claude is a successful regional sales manager based in Dubai, working for a US Fortune top 500 company. His direct team covers all of the Middle-East and North-Africa. I once asked him what makes him successful in sales. He answered "Knowledge. Knowledge commends respect. My prospects perceive me as such a knowledgeable person. You will rarely come across an ignorant customer in the 21st century, because anyone can spend a few minutes online and tell you exactly how much you should charge for a product or a service. I make sure I share enough information and knowledge with my customers so they open up, and that ultimately leads to closing a deal. This also means I prepare well before entering the meeting so the information sharing process is also a process where I get to share the value-added of my offering." This statement tells us all we need to know about being regarded as a "consultant", rather than a "regular sales representative."

Pointer 2: Deal closing skills

So, what do you do after you have handled all the prospect's objections and sensed his readiness to move forward? Do you say "Thank you for the meeting, it was great chatting with you. Be in touch. Bye"? Or do you sit there with your fingers crossed hoping the customer will tell you "OK, I am ready to close the deal, let's do this"? None. Remember the purpose of you being there: closing the deal. Having a friendly meeting with a prospect is great. But sales people don't get commissions based on how friendly their sales meetings were. They get

例如：

我相信我们已经协商过各个方面的问题了，我们可以成交了吗？

我们已经讨论过产品 A 和产品 B 了，您希望我们为您提供哪一款？

我们想与您合作，现在我们需要做些什么来启动这个项目呢？

我最喜欢的是最后一个。几年前我在美国得克萨斯州的休斯敦租房子的时候用的就是这个方法。我沿着威斯海姆大街参观了几个房子和公寓，最后参观的那个房子就是我后来选定的地方。那是一个周五的下午，我已经在不同的社区参观十多个房子了，我想快点结束，但又不能表现得太明显而让销售代表看出来，否则这一点就会在谈判过程中被他利用。这名销售代表是雷伊先生，他是一名既幽默又有礼貌的男士。他带我参观他们的房产，向我展示社区，为我解释租赁价格并回应了我的所有担忧。但他并没有在那时完成交易。在我们回到他的办公室之后，他把我带到会议室，给我提供了一杯饮品，让我稍等一会儿。两分钟过后，他的经理带着一份文件走了进来，以下是我们的谈话过程：

经理：您好，阿道先生，我是雷伊的经理，这是一份合同。我知道您很喜欢我们的房产和社区。在签订这份合同前，您还需要我们为您做什么？

我：我今天早上参观了 Briar Bend 公园附近的一套公寓，很不错。他们提供的带阳台的公寓跟你们这套差不多，月租费比你们便宜 100 美元，所以我需要再考虑一下。

经理：仅仅是价格上的问题，还是说您有其他的需求想要告诉我呢？

我：目前来看主要是价格的问题。

经理：如果您现在可以承诺签 12 个月的租期的话，我可以给出与他们同样的价格。我之所以可以给出这样的条件是因为这个月才刚开始，我还能够给你上个月的报价，明天的话就不会再有这样的价格了。

我：我觉得这个价格可以接受。

commissions based on how many deals they closed. If you have assessed the needs, made an offer, and handled all the prospect's objections, then ask the prospect to close the deal. As simple as that. You can say it either directly or indirectly, depending on the personality of the prospect you have been negotiating with.

Examples:

I believe we have covered all the aspects. Do we have a deal?

We have discussed product A and product B. Which one would you like us to deliver?

We want to do business with you. What can we do to begin working on this project now?

This last one is my favorite. It was used on me a few years ago when I was looking for a place to rent in Houston, State of Texas. I visited several houses and apartments along Westheimer Avenue, and the last one was the one that I settled for. It was a Friday afternoon and I had already visited more than a dozen houses in different neighborhoods. I needed that process to be over, but of course I didn't make it obvious to the sales representative so it won't be used against me during the negotiation. The sales representative, Mr. Rey, was a likeable guy with great attitude and good humor. He took me around their property, showed me around the neighborhood, explained the rental prices, and responded to all my concerns. But he didn't close the deal. When we returned to his office, he walked me to the meeting room, offered me a drink, and asked me to wait for a moment. Two minutes later, his manager walked in with a file in her hand and the discussion developed as follows.

Manager: Hi Mr. Benkerroum! I'm Rey's manager, and I have the contract with me here. I understand you like our property and our neighborhood. What exactly do you need from us to be able to sign this contract right now?

Me: I have visited this morning a nice apartment off Stoney Brook Drive next to Briar Bend Park. They are offering exactly similar units with balcony at a monthly rate that's 100 USD cheaper than yours. So I need to think it over.

Manager: Is it just a pricing issue or is there any other need that you would like to tell me about?

最好的成交要么关乎时间期限，要么就是一种优惠刺激。该经理的成交两者均包含。对我来说，她报出的那个只在当天有效的价格，不管是不是虚张声势都对我没什么影响。我甚至不会觉得进一步的商谈有什么压迫感。她给了我我所需要的，同时我也给了她她想要的东西。她以一种令人赞叹的方式处理好了我们之间的交流。作为回报，她也获得了我这笔生意。

在我离开之前，我告诉她我喜欢该社区里的一家健身房，并问她是否碰巧认识那里的某个人。她给我推荐了一个联系人，因为她认识老板，我获得了在这个健身房免费试用一个月的机会。

当你尝试完成交易的时候，潜在客户要么接受，并像我租公寓那次一样继续推进这笔交易，要么犹豫并拒绝，或者保持沉默。

在你打算完成交易的时候如果潜在客户保持沉默的话，你该做什么？很简单，闭嘴别多话。你已经问了问题而潜在客户正在思考，那就给他思考的时间。当沉默开始变得尴尬时，喝一小口水，并在你的笔记本上做笔记，这在谈判的任一阶段都是行得通的。举个例子来说，在你报出价格之后，潜在客户什么话都不说地盯着你，这时候，不要打破沉默。这是对方的一个谈判策略，而这个策略正在你身上施行。保持镇静，保持沉默。

提示 3: 如何应对在即将完成交易时客户说“不”的情形

那么在你打算完成交易的时候潜在客户却说“不”，你又该怎么做？

你应该时刻牢记成交只是时间上的问题。如果在阻力应对阶段你遗漏了一些购买阻力，那它们又会在交易的最后阶段重新出现。在这种情况下，试着找出潜在客户仍然犹豫不决的原因，然后再次尝试在结束交易前解决这些

Me: At this stage, it's mostly a matter of price.

Manager: If you commit to a 12-month lease now, I will match their prices. I can only make this offer because today is the very beginning of the month, so I will still be able to extend last month's prices to you. This offer won't be valid tomorrow.

Me: I think we can go with that.

The best closings are tied to a timeline or to an incentive. Hers contained both. It didn't matter to me whether she was bluffing or not when she said that the price was valid just for that day. I didn't even feel compelled to negotiate further. She gave me what I wanted, and in return I gave her what she wanted. She handled the interaction in an impressive manner. As a reward, she got my business.

Before I left, I told her about a gym in the neighborhood that I liked, and asked if she happened to know someone there that I could talk to. She recommended a contact, and I got a 1-month free trial at the gym because she knew the owner.

When you attempt to close, the prospect will either accept and proceed like I did with the apartment, or show hesitation and say no, or stay quiet.

What to do if you attempt to close and the prospect stays quiet? It's simple. Shut up. Do not add anything. You have asked a question and the prospect is thinking. So let him think. When the silence starts feeling awkward, take a sip of water and scribble notes on your notebook. This is to be used at any stage of the negotiation. If, for example, you announce your price, and the prospect just stares at you without saying a thing, the same rule applies: Don't break the silence. It's a negotiation tactic and it's being used against you. Stay calm and keep quiet.

Pointer 3: How to deal with a prospect who says "No" during the closing phase

And what to do if you attempt to close but the prospect says "no"?

You should always remember that closing is all about timing. If there are some objections that you omitted to handle during the Objections Handling phase,

购买阻力。当你想结束交易时问问自己："如果我没能成功完成这次交易，会发生的最糟糕的事情是什么？"答案是："什么都不会发生。"他们说了"不"，而你也只是回到了购买阻力的发掘阶段。或许你的提案原本就不完全匹配他们的需求，那么他们的拒绝反而是件好事。**客户拒绝一个无法满足其需求的产品要比买下后对你满怀抱怨好得多。**

如果所有的条件都还不足以让你完成交易，应向潜在客户发出第二次会面的邀请，并在那时再做进一步的协商。以下两种方式是有区别的：

离开销售会议时告诉潜在客户："我会把你需要的信息搜集给你，并尽快重新安排一次会谈。"

打开你的日程表，放在桌上，然后告诉客户："我会在 3 天内给您反馈这方面的信息，你下周哪天有空？我们再一起聊聊。"

现在你大概已经尝试过所有的技巧了，但还是无法完成交易。那么，是时候和你的管理层进行沟通了，找找到底是因为什么而不能成功地完成交易。你可能会发现你的价格太过离谱，这使你永远无法获得成交。或者你可能会发现你的产品欠缺潜在客户要求具备的功能。如果是这样，马上与你的直属经理沟通，并试着找出那些可以改进的部分，以此提升你的成交概率。

提示 4: 面对未成交，以积极的方式结束

在进行到下个步骤前还有最后一件事需要注意，那就是在你试着结束交易时不要表现得太过强势。当你试图压迫性地推销你的东西时，对方往往会与你激烈对抗。你要明白不是所有的交易都会以成交收场。如果你已经找出并解决了所有的购买阻力，但还是没有获得成交，可以用以下积极的方式结束：

then those objections will resurface when you are attempting to finalize the deal at the Closing phase. In this case, try to identify the reason why the prospect is still hesitant, and address those objections before attempting to close again. When you want to close, ask yourself "What is the worst that could happen if I try to close and don't succeed". The answer is "nothing". They will just say "no" and you go back to objections uncovering. Maybe the offer you made does not exactly match their needs, in which case their refusal to close the deal is a good sign. **It's better to have a customer refusing to buy a product that doesn't work for them, than having them buy it and flood you with complaints**.

If all the conditions are not there yet for you to close, make sure you ask the prospect for a second meeting where you will be able to take the discussion further. There is a difference between:

Leaving a sales meeting telling the prospect: "I'll get you the information you asked me about and we will schedule a meeting again soon".

And opening your agenda, putting it on the table, and saying: "I'll be able to get this information within maximum three days and come back for a follow-up meeting next week. How does your schedule look like beginning of next week?"

Now, you might have tried all the techniques, but you still can not close the deal. If so, then it is time to sit down with your management and figure out why you are failing to close. You might find out that your prices are massively out of whack, in which case you will never be able to close. Or you might find out that the product is lacking a feature the prospects always request. Get with your direct manager quickly and try to figure out what areas you can work on to improve your closing rate.

Pointer 4: Ending on a positive note, even when the deal doesn't materialize

A last thing to add here before moving on to the next step.Do not be too

- 感谢潜在客户能花时间与你会面交谈；
- 让潜在客户知道你会在几周后再次与其联系；
- 询问潜在客户是否能够把你介绍给某个他认识的，或许会对你的产品感兴趣的人；
- 邀请潜在客户参加你公司将于几周后举办的一次活动；
- 请求将潜在客户加为你和你公司社交媒体账号的联系人。

aggressive when you try to close. People are likely to respond aggressively if you try to shove things down their throat. Understand that not all deals will end up with a closing. If you have uncovered and addressed all the objections, and yet you can't have a deal, leave in positive terms by:

■ Thanking the prospect for the time spent with you.

■ Letting the prospect know that you will get back in touch again in a few weeks.

■ Asking the prospect if he can put you in touch with someone he knows who might be interested in your product.

■ Inviting the prospect to an event your company is organizing in the coming weeks.

■ Asking the prospect to connect with you and your company on social media.

成交后还有哪些事情需要做

销售会议刚一结束，所有人都如释重负。在结束会议并回到办公室后，你做的第一件事是什么呢？

提示1：未成交也可以获得有用信息

你或许会认为销售流程在完成销售会议后就结束了，其实不然。实际上，只要你还在和潜在客户联系，你就仍然处于销售会议之中，即使你已经被潜在客户送出门。在你离开会议室向着出口走去的时候，问问潜在客户“我真的觉得这款产品很符合您的需求，您可以告诉我您选择不购买的原因是什么吗”也无妨。因为谈判已经结束了，并且你也已经走出了会议室，潜在客户可能是愿意和你分享这个信息的，特别是当会议进行时他的同事或经理在场

Follow-up

Everybody feels relieved once the sales meeting is over. What is the first thing you do as soon as you finish your meeting and get back to your office?

Pointer 1: You can still get valuable information, even if you don't get the deal

You might think that the sales process ends when the sales meeting is over. It does not. In fact, as long as you are interacting with the prospect, you are still in the sales meeting, even when the prospect is walking you out through the door. When you are leaving the meeting room, and heading towards the exit door, you don't lose anything by asking the prospect "I really thought this product was a fit for your needs. Can you let me know why you decided not to buy?" Because the negotiation is over, and you are out of the meeting room, the prospect might feel inclined to

的情况下。

提示 2: 给你的潜在客户发送一封总结性的邮件

如果你在离开销售会议的时候获得了成交，那么恭喜你！这时你要整理好参会时所做的笔记并给所有的参会者发送电子邮件。这件事需要你在回到办公室后尽快完成，别太拖延！在这份总结性的邮件中：

- 感谢潜在客户的赴会；
- 总结你们协商过的要点；
- 列出要推进的后续步骤（合同、业务表格、样品等）；
- 以“如有遗漏的地方，还请麻烦您告诉我好吗”结尾。

最后一句话非常重要。通过在结尾提问，你可能从对方那儿获得一个答复。一旦他回复了你的电子邮件，这就意味着他已经阅读了你的总结，并知晓了邮件的内容。将来当你再次遇到这个人而他的记忆出现差错时，你就可以向他展示你的随访邮件以及他的确认。而那时他就不能再说“抱歉，我还没来得及阅读上次你发给我的电子邮件”了。

提示 3: 让潜在客户回复你的随访邮件与发送这封邮件同样重要

我曾遇到过这样一个情况，我的一个潜在客户在与我会面的几天后“辞职”了。她实际上是被解雇的，这意味着她留下烂摊子后就走了，也没有把她所有的项目交接给新雇员。她的经理当时也不知道她和我会过面，所以我们就只能把所有的流程重新走一遍。如果那时我能及时地获得一封确认

share that information with you, especially if the meeting was taking place in the presence of his colleagues or managers.

Pointer 2: Send a summary email to the prospect

If you leave the sales meeting and you did close the deal, congratulations! Now make sure you reorganize the notes from the meeting and send an email to all of the participants. That should be done as soon as you get back to your office. Don't let it drag! In that recap email:

- Thank the prospect for their time.
- Summarize the points you discussed.
- List the next steps moving forward (contract, forms, samples, etc).
- End the email by "Could you please let me know if I have missed anything in my email?"

That last statement is very important. By asking a question at the end, you are trying to secure a response from your counterpart. Once he responds to your email, it means that he has read your summary and acknowledges its content. Later on, if you meet with that same person again and he experiences a memory lapse, you can show him your follow-up email as well as his acknowledgments. He has no way to say "Sorry, I didn't get a chance to read the email you sent last time".

Pointer 3: Getting the prospect to answer your follow-up email is as important as sending that follow-up

I had a case where a prospect "left" her job a few days after meeting with me. She was actually fired, which means she left her position in bad terms and without transitioning all her projects to the new comer. Her manager was not aware of the meeting she had with me, and we had to go through the process all over

邮件的话，就可以直接在该邮件内容的基础上和那家公司进一步商谈了。幸运的是，他们对此足够包容，所以很快就又进行到了那位雇员离职前的步骤。

这种总结性的邮件可以告诉潜在客户两件事：第一，你在他讲话的时候的确认真在听；第二，他可以依靠你梳理的信息向前推进项目。我的前经理克里斯·丹尼尔森总会向我强调第二点。我在刚开始写这本书的时候就联系过他，跟他聊了聊关于他在处理数百万美元级别客户上的个人经验，而第二点又再次被提到了。当我问他是什么让他在工作中如此成功时，他答道："执行力就是一切。这是与客户建立信任的第一步。如果你承诺了要做什么，你就必须执行，并从一开始就做好后续跟进。"

你不一定要将这个邮件写成一本书，有几个要点就足够了，否则没人会阅读你的电子邮件。

除了发送跟进邮件以外，有必要花些时间反思一下这次会议，想想什么可能对你的成交有所帮助，或者什么可能会导致你的成交失败。如果你是和一名同事一起参加销售会议的，那你的个人评估就简单得多了，因为你们可以就这次会议的表现互相交换想法，可以知道自己在哪些方面做得好，哪些方面需要在下次加以改善。

提示 4: 不断与老客户拓展业务

寻求一名新客户的代价是很高的，而回到现有的客户那儿，为他们提供更多的产品并拓展业务的话，对你的公司来说可能更加有利。在成交后，会出现一个完全不同的流程：客户维护，它是可以最大化进行交叉销售的机会，通过客户维护过程在同一个特定的客户身上探寻额外的盈利。我不想把它包

again. If I had secured a confirmation to my email just on time, I could have used that as a basis for my future discussions with that company. Luckily, they were accommodating enough to move quickly and build-up on the previous discussion.

The recap email tells the prospect two things: one, that you were actually listening when he was talking; and the other, that he can count on your discipline moving forward. This second point has always been highlighted to me by my former manager Kris Danielson. I contacted him when I started writing this book to have a chat over his experience servicing multi-million dollar customers. And that point came back again. When I asked him what makes him successful in his job, he said that "Execution is everything. It is the first step of building that trust with the customer. If you say you will do something, you must execute and follow-up right from the beginning."

You don't have to write a book. A few bullet points will suffice. Otherwise no one will read your email.

Besides sending the follow-up email, it is always worth it to take some time to reflect on the meeting, and what might have contributed in closing the deal, or losing it. If you go to the sales meeting with a colleague, then that personal assessment is made easier as it allows for an exchange of ideas on what you have done well and where you will need to improve next time.

Pointer 4: Don't stop expanding business with acquired customers

Acquiring a new customer is costly. But going back to an existing customer to offer more products and expand the business can turn out to be more beneficial for your company. After closing the deal, a whole different process kicksin. It's called the Retention Process. It consists of maximizing cross-sell opportunities and exploring additional revenue opportunities with the same specific customers by having a retention program. I didn't want to include under the umbrella of "Follow-up Phase" because I

含在“后续跟进阶段”的内容里，因为我不想降低其重要性。它远超出了一个基本的后续跟进的范围。

四年前，我的一个朋友因为她的贸易公司销售额严重下滑而联系我。他们试着依靠曾经适用的老方法：投入更多的金钱，雇用更多的员工……然后袖手旁观等着情况恢复正常。但是，这样做并不会让这家公司恢复正常。我花了些时间对他们的各个流程进行检视后发现，他们很明显把焦点都放在了寻找新客户上，而完全没有探寻现有客户的潜在价值。总的来说，他们每次刚与一名新客户完成交易，就又开始寻找新客户。除了每年给老客户发一次新年祝福邮件外，他们完全没有维护过这些老客户。和我的这位朋友交谈过后，我建议做个实验。其内容是根据他们销售团队人员的知识和个性差异将他们分为两组：猎人组和农民组。然后我们分别给两组提供清晰的职位描述，以此确保他们两组都明白自己的定位以及了解新的分组将在未来几个月如何影响他们的行为。猎人组的定位是极具活力的销售代表，寻觅新生意并获得成交是他们的唯一职责。他们的任务很简单：敲门、会面、谈判、成交、重复、重复、再重复。

一旦获得了成交，该客户就会被转移至农民组，而农民组的唯一职责便是去“养护”与客户的关系。农民组是关系建立者，他们必须照料好这些已经在公司接受过一次服务的客户。我们决定把这些现有的客户称为“家人和朋友”，以此强调我们所致力于实现的关系水平。农民组有一个明确的任务：去调动客户，愉悦客户，并以建立信任和提升客户对我们的依赖度为目标维护好现有的客户。一周后，我们从“家人和朋友”那儿获得了两个新订单。一个月后，我们从“家人和朋友”那儿获得了 11 个新订单，以及 1 份正在商谈的关于将一名现有客户转变为朋友公司在客户所在国家的独家代理的合同。

don't want to minimize its importance. It goes beyond a basic follow-up.

Four years ago, a friend of mine contacted me because her trading company was looking at its sales volumes dropping at a frightening pace. They tried to recover by relying on the old method that had worked in the past: throw more money at it, and hire more people, then sit back… things will get back in order. Newsflash: Nothing got back in order. After spending some time going through their processes, it was obvious to me that they all talked about seeking new customers, but no mention was made of exploring the potential with existing ones. Basically, once they concluded their transaction with a new customer, they moved on to look for a new one. The existing customers were not engaged at all, except for an email that they sent to old customers once a year to wish them a Happy New Year. After a chat with my friend, I suggested we start an experiment. It consisted of splitting their sales team into two distinct groups, depending on their knowledge and their personalities: The Hunters and The Farmers. We then defined a clear job description for each group to make sure they both knew where they stood and how this new split would affect their activity for the months to follow. The Hunters were extremely dynamic sales representatives whose only task was to hunt down new businesses and close deals. Their mission was simple: knock on doors, meet, negotiate, close the deal, repeat, repeat, and repeat.

As soon as the deal was closed, the customer was passed over to the Farmers whose only task was to "cultivate" that relationship. The Farmers were relationship builders, and they had to take care of those customers that the company had already serviced once. We decided to call those existing customers "family and friends" in order to emphasize the level of relationship we were aiming for. The Farmers had one clear mission: to engage, delight, and sustain existing customers with the aim of building trust and increasing interdependency between them and us. One week into the program, we had secured two new orders from the "family and friends". One month into the program, we had 11 new orders from our "family and friends", and one contract in negotiation to turn an existing customer into an exclusive agent in their country.

回看这些天，我不觉得我们创造了奇迹。我们只是重新分配了资源，并在导向成功的轨道上设立了团队。一旦他们走上正轨，他们就会成功。

留住客户在各种情况下都非常有意义，开发新客户的成本要远远高于维护现有客户。通过维护你的现有客户，你将会发现他们当中有一些未被开发的潜力是你之前没有意识到的。只有建立了关系和信任才能发掘出这种潜力。

我坚信客户维护的力量，而这或许会是我另外一本书的主题。

但是现在，让我们先来探索一些经过验证的谈判技巧，并以此进入谈判的核心部分吧。

Looking back at those days, I don't believe we did any miracles. We just re-allocated resources, and set the team on a track to succeed. Once they were put on that track, they did succeed.

Customer retention makes lots of sense in many circumstances, because acquiring new customers is more costly than nurturing the existing ones. By nurturing your existing customers, you will find out that some of them have untapped potential that you were not aware of. Only relationship and trust building can reveal that potential.

I strongly believe in the power of customer retention. That might be the topic of another book.

But for now, let's get down to the heart of negotiation by exploring some proven negotiation tactics.

阿道的独家谈判策略

每个谈判都是独一无二的，其结果与参与方的个性、谈判的地点、文化差异、一天中的哪个时刻或一周中的哪一天会面等各个方面有着极大的关系。没有人能百分之百地准确预测谈判的进展。即使如此，你还是必须做好使用正确的谈判策略的准备，这样才能够让其帮助并指引你在谈判的过程中向“成交”这个目标一步步推进。

我在本书中列出了 10 项最常用到的谈判策略，你既可以在采购或销售的时候用，也可以在生活中的其他谈判场景中使用，比如在和你的孩子或者你的经理谈判的时候。“策略”一词的英文“tactic”来源于希腊语“taktike”，其含义是“约定的艺术”，而这恰恰是谈判的意义所在。

你会发现我在本书中提到的一些谈判策略不是完全“高尚”的。我强烈建议你千万不要把它们用于跟其他组织建立有意义的关系上。我之所以在这里提到这一条的原因是希望在对方拿这些来对付你的时候，你能察觉到。

策略 1：低球技巧

这个策略是让你在开始的时候提出一个非常有诱惑力的报价，一旦对方同意，再借机加价。这个策略由 3 个阶段组成：

- 卖家提出一个非常有诱惑力的报价；
- 买家同意交易，甚至已经签订合同或者支付一笔定金；
- 卖家对提案稍做修改，但这个修改足够小以至于不会使买家改变主意。

Abdel's ultimate negotiation tactics

Every negotiation is unique. Its outcome depends largely on the personalities of the parties involved, the location where it takes place, the cultural differences, the time of the day or of the week, and so many other variables. No one can predict with a 100% accuracy how the negotiation will develop. However, one can and must be prepared to use the right negotiation tactics that will help him guide the flow of the negotiation towards the "We have a deal" moment.

I am listing in this book 10 of the most used negotiation tactics that you can use either when buying/selling, or in other negotiation situations from your life such as a negotiation with your kid or with your manager. The word "tactic" derives from the Greek word "taktike", which means "the art of arrangement". And that's what negotiation is all about.

You will find that some of the negotiation tactics I'm relating in this book are purely unethical. I highly advise you against using them if you want to build a meaningful relationship with the other party. The only reason why I'm relating them here is so you are aware of them in case they get used against you.

Tactic 1: Low-balling

This tactic consists of opening with a fantastic offer, but once the other party agrees, other necessities emerge. This tactic develops in 3 phases:

- The seller makes a very attractive offer.
- The buyer agrees to the deal and might even sign the contract or make a deposit payment.
- The seller slightly changes his offer, but with a change small enough that will not make the buyer back out.

在我们做进一步的探讨之前，先快速地了解一下“有诱惑力的报价”。当一个报价非常有诱惑力时，它往往隐含着某个问题或者条件。当某样东西好得不太现实时，可能就会出现这种状况，要在交易的过程中保持警惕。

比如说你正准备采购一台机器来支持企业的生产。你找到了一款特别匹配的机器而且价格非常合适。你刚和机器的制造商谈妥了价格，他们就告诉你安装的费用需要你额外支付。因为价格很低，你就同意了。等你付了钱，你又发现还需要为培训员工使用机器再额外支付一笔费用。这样的问题后续还有很多。

有一个现实生活中的例子，也是相同的道理：邀请你的朋友明天一起去爬山。一旦你的朋友接受并答应，你再加一句“还有就是，巴士早上六点出发”。如果你提前告诉他出发时间，他或许会拒绝。但现在他既然已经答应，再退出的概率就会低很多。

还有一个策略也叫**低球技巧**，但和刚才所说的不太一样。买家在用这个策略时会先提出一个极低的价格。价格低到足以让你感到被冒犯。千万别掉到这个陷阱里。用此方法的买家是想通过你的情绪反应，来辨别你是否对自己所销售产品的价值有充分的认识。如果你碰到对方使用这样的策略，只需再次重复你的价格，并在谈话毫无进展时做好离开的准备。

我个人回应该策略的方式虽有些激进，却能够让买家明白，如果他不是认真要买我的产品，那就不应该浪费我的时间。比如说我正在以 3 万美元的价格出售我的汽车，一名潜在买家给我打电话并报出 1 万美元这样荒唐的价格。我会用一种更为荒诞的方式回应他：“不好意思，我在发布价格的时候出了点差错，我实际上的报价是 4 万美元。”

Before we move forward, Let's take a quick look at "attractive offers." When an offer is very attractive, it is likely that there is a problem or a condition hidden somewhere. If something is too good to be true, it probably is. Be very attentive as the transaction develops.

Let's say you are looking into buying a machine to support your production. You find the exact machine you were looking for at a very good price. Once you talk to the manufacturer and agree on a price, you will be told that you have to pay additional fees for the installation. You agree to that because those are very low. Once you pay, you will learn that there are additional training charges to train your employees on how to use the machine. This game can keep going on and on.

An example of this in the real life would be to tell your friend that you should go mountain-climbing tomorrow together for ×× reason. Once the friend accepts and commits, you will add a "by the way, the bus leaves at 6 am". If you have told him the timing upfront, he might have refused. But now that he has already committed, the chances of backing out are lower.

There is another tactic different from this one, but that is also called **Low-balling**. In this tactic, the buyer will open with a very low price. So ridiculously low that will make the seller feel almost insulted. Don't fall for this one. The buyer is looking for an emotional reaction from you to identify if you (the seller) are well informed about the value of what you are selling. If this tactic is used against you, just repeat your price again, and be prepared to walk away if the discussion is going nowhere.

The way I personally respond to that tactic is a bit more radical, but it sends a message to the buyer that he shouldn't waste my time if he is not serious about buying. Say, for example, I'm in the process of selling my car for the price of 30,000 USD, a potential buyer calls me and offers the outrageous price of 10,000 USD. I would just counter with an even more outrageous one by saying "Sorry, I have made a mistake when I posted the price. I'm actually asking for 40,000 USD".

策略 2: 还价

当你接受对方提案的一些或大部分条件，要修改其中的一部分时，一个还价的机会就出现了。它一般是这样的："如果你给我们（确切的某样东西），我们就会考虑给你（不确切的某样东西）。"这种方式听起来不怎么出彩，但确实有用。你一定经常听到一些人这么说："如果你答应在 2 天内交货，我们会重新考虑给价格加几个百分点。"这是一个标准的谈判策略，试试也无妨。你甚至还可以这样还价："要不你把你的价格降 10%，我们再想办法来加快配送过程？"其关键在于对对方的要求要具体，对我方的要求可以不那么具体。

策略 3: 唱红脸，唱白脸

这个策略也称为"联合审讯"。我们都看过犯罪嫌疑人被逮捕并被带到警察局的那些电影。犯罪嫌疑人坐在审讯室里，然后一个凶狠且有威慑力的警察走进来，该警察试着用恐吓的方式来让他招供。然后"坏警察"出去，又走进来一个和善的警察。该犯罪嫌疑人会因为"坏警察"而情绪异常激动，而友善的警察则会让刚刚还拒绝招供的犯罪嫌疑人敞开心扉。"好警察"扮演的是暂时与犯罪嫌疑人同一阵线的善意施助者的角色。一旦他从犯罪嫌疑人那儿得到自己想要的东西后，就会站起来离开。这是在现实中真实发生的事，它其实就是一个心理游戏。

在销售过程中，在买方有两名代表参加会议的情况下可以使用这个策略。其中一人扮演无理又顽固的角色，另一人则扮演包容又和善的角色。另一种

Tactic 2: Counteroffer

A counteroffer happens when accepting some or most of the terms of the other party's offer, but modifying some others. It goes something like this: "If you give us (something specific), we will explore giving you (something not specific)". Put that way, it sounds dull. But it works. How many times you have heard someone saying something like "If you accept to deliver the goods within the coming 2 days, we will reconsider Increasing our price by a few percentages". This is a standard negotiation tactic and there is no harm in using it. You could even counter a counteroffer by saying something like "How about you decrease your prices by 10%, and we will see what we can do to speed up the delivery?" The key is to request something specific while offering something that is not.

Tactic 3: Bad Cop / Good Cop Routine

This is also called "Joint Questioning". We all have watched those movies where a suspect is arrested and taken to the police station. He is sitting at the interrogation room, and a mean and threatening cop walks in. The cop tries to intimidate the suspect to make him recognize the facts. The "bad cop" then walks out, and a nicer cop walks in. The suspect will be so emotionally charged against the "bad cop", that the appearance of a "friendly" face will make him give away what he was refusing to give away just a moment ago. The good cop plays the role of the nice and supportive guy who is siding with the suspect momentarily. As soon as he gets what he wants from the suspect, he stands-up and walks away. This actually happens in reality, and it is just a mind game.

In sales, it is practiced when two people from the buyer's side walk into the meeting. One person plays the role of the unreasonable tough guy, and the other plays the role of the accommodating friendly guy. Another variance is having the"bad

情况是让“红脸”角色先参与会议，然后以接电话或参加其他会议为由离开，接着“白脸”角色进来。

你应该意识到那两个人早在和你会面之前就已经串通好了，这是一个心理游戏。“红脸”角色是为“白脸”角色做铺垫的，从而使后者看起来既讲道理又友好。你是否曾遇到过这样的情况，当你想在一家商店里买点什么东西时，那儿的销售代表试着给你一些折扣，然而她的老板却怨她怎么可以给这么多的折扣？是的，这就是一个“唱红脸，唱白脸”的策略！

回看我个人在销售方面的经历，我发现扮演“白脸”的人要么是律师，要么是会计。这是巧合？我并不这么认为。

那么我该如何回应这个策略呢？我假装自己不知道，只有在感到谈话变得失控的情况下才会反击。如果是那样的话，我的回答分为买家版和卖家版。如果我是买家，我会如实说：“我知道你们在干什么，你们在对我唱红白脸，我不是来和你们搭戏的。是否可以认真点，看看能否达成对双方都有利的一致意见。”并且，我在说这番的时候，会全程保持微笑。

如果我是卖家，我会表现出情绪并责怪唱红脸的人误导会议的方向。我可以假装生气并要求暂作小憩来舒缓压力。

策略 4: 沉默

沉默是一个非常强大的工具。在谈判过程中使用这个策略会使对方不自在，特别是在对方很健谈的情况下。中国的谈判者非常擅长使用这个策略。当你刚宣布完价格或在你面对一个困难处境的时候，使用该策略会有强大的效果。困难处境有可能是潜在买家想让你做出的一个让步。以下便是一个典型的例子：

guy" starting the meeting, then leaving to supposedly receive a call or join another meeting. Then the "nice guy" comes in to the table.

You should be aware that those two have already coordinated their actions before meeting with you. It's a mind game. The bad guy's role is to set up the good guy to seem reasonable and friendly. Have you ever been in a situation where you wanted to buy something at a shop, and the sales representative was trying to give you some discount, whereas her boss was arguing that she is discounting so much? Well, that's a "Bad Cop / Good Cop" Routine right there!

Looking back at my personal experience in sales, it turns out that most of the "bad guys" roles I have witnessed were played by either lawyers or accountants. A coincidence? I think not.

How do I respond to that? I play along as if I'm not aware of the trick. I will fire back only if I feel that the discussion is getting out of hand. In that case, my response depends on whether I'm the buyer or the seller. If I'm the buyer, I call it what it is: "I see what you're trying to do here. You're playing the Bad Cop/Good Cop Routine on me. I'm not here to play games. How about we get serious and work on reaching an agreement that will benefit all of us?" All done with a smile.

If I'm a seller, I would get emotional, and blame the bad cop for the direction the meeting is taking. I can pretend to be angry and then ask to take a break to diffuse tension.

Tactic 4: Silence

Silence is a very powerful tool. When used during the course of a negotiation, it makes the other party uncomfortable, especially if that other party is talkative by nature. Chinese negotiators are very good at using this tactic. It has a stronger effect when used right after announcing the price or when confronted with a tough situation. That tough situation could be a concession that a potential buyer is asking you to make. An example of how this can evolve:

Buyer: I would like to ask for a better price on your Premium package.

买家：我希望你能给我一个更好的高级套餐价格。

卖家：（沉默几秒）。

买家：如果这个要求太过分，那就算了。

你会吃惊地发现当人们面对几秒钟的沉默时，他们会多么一致地收回之前的请求或做出让步。如果他们没有这么做，他们往往也会在交谈中提出一些能够帮你做决定的额外信息，即使这些信息和让步或请求并没有什么直接的联系。这是因为我们习惯于让自己的感官一直都有事可做：听音乐、看电视、玩手机、被喧闹的人群环绕等。一旦我们感受到场景被沉默所占据，我们就会试着在情况变得更为尴尬之前用说话来填补这些空白。

这在谈判中被称为"谁先说话，谁就输了"。大部分情况都是如此，只有少数几种情况下你可以打破沉默，我会在后面的部分谈到。

当谈判对方用这种策略对付你时，你可以做以下几件事情：

- 通过重申你刚刚说过的内容来打破沉默，比如一个价格或声明；
- 喝一小口水并在你的笔记本上做记录；
- 面对谈判方并说："你不说话，我也不说话。"
- 如果沉默时间过长，那就要求暂作休息；
- 在保持眼神交流的同时，展现你沉默而高深莫测的微笑；
- 告诉对方如果他们没有什么要补充的，建议可以结束会议（这是最后的选择）。

至于要保持沉默多久，这并没有什么规则。一般情况下，你会在每个人都保持沉默之后的 4 到 5 秒开始感到空气中弥漫的焦虑气息。对这种焦虑和紧张免疫的唯一方式就是练习。下次有人叫你去做什么事或者向你要什么东西时，保持几秒钟的沉默并试着不要去打破它。多重复几次这样的练习，直到你开始觉得沉默也可以成为你最好的朋友为止。

Seller: (Silence for a few seconds).

Buyer: If this is too much asking, then it's okay.

You will be surprised by how many times people will retract their request or make a concession when confronted with a few seconds of silence. If they don't, it is likely that they will volunteer additional information that can help you in the discussion, even if it's not directly related to a concession or a request. This is because we are used to having our senses engaged all the time, listening to music, watching TV, playing with the phone, being surrounded by a noisy crowd…etc. As soon as we feel that a silence is taking hold of a situation, we try to talk to fill those voids before the situation gets more awkward.

In negotiations, it is said that "He who speaks first, loses". This is generally true, but you can break that silence in a few cases that I will discuss in the coming pages.

When the other party used this tactic against you, there are a few things you could do:

- Break the silence by restating what you have just said, being it a price or a statement.
- Take a sip of your water and take notes on your notebook.
- Break the silence by confronting the other party and saying "I can be quiet just as long as you can".
- Ask for a break if the silence seems too exaggerated.
- Put on a silence and enigmatic smile, all while keeping eye-contact.
- Tell the other party that if they don't have anything to add, you suggest to end the meeting (this is a last resort solution).

As to how long to keep that silence going, there is no rule. Generally, you will start feeling the agitation in the air for 4 to 5 seconds after everyone is quiet. The only way to build immunity against that agitation or tension is to practice. Next time someone asks you to do or give something, stay quiet for a few seconds and try not

策略 5: 夸夸其谈

就是向对方提供远超出其承受能力的大量信息。这些信息可以包含说明、需求、数据、事实等，所有信息均以错乱的条理和方式对其展示。这么做的目的一是争取时间，二是延迟对方重整策略并做出决定的时间。这么做可以使对方困惑，让对方很难分辨哪些信息是真实的，哪些是重要的，哪些是分散注意力的。

如果某个潜在客户用这种策略对付你，那就要求分次进行会议并分别安排技术专家用以处理交易中的相应部分。如果文件过于冗长，那就对具体的问题进行提问，并询问对方可以在文件的哪一部分找到相应的答案。

策略 6: 虚假让步

虚假让步是指你在谈判时将某样东西给予对方，而这些给予的东西其实并非是你在意的，你只是想通过放弃这些本就不重要的东西来获得真正想要的回报。一个在工作场所经常被提及的例子是：有一名员工请求提薪和获得一个额外的带薪假期。这里的带薪假期就是一个虚假让步。在谈判的过程中，该员工会放弃假期请求并专注于加薪。情况是这样的，该员工放弃了他本来就不想要的东西，而同时获得了他真正感兴趣和原本就想要的东西。在使用这个策略时一定要格外小心，因为有可能适得其反。他的雇主也可能会同意给他一个额外的带薪假期而拒绝他的提薪请求，要做好发生这种情况的准备。

现在，在讨论下一点之前，我想就让步的问题来做一些澄清。在谈判中，让步**不是给予**，而是**交易**。你无须付出什么，除非你获得回报。这叫

to break the silence. Repeat this again for a few times until you start realizing that silence could be your best friend.

Tactic 5: Snow Job

It consists of flooding the other party with more information than they can possibly analyze. It can consist of figures, demands, data, facts…all presented in a disorganized manner. The goal here is to buy more time and delay a decision in order to refocus one's strategy. It confuses the other party in a way that makes it difficult for them to identify what's real, what's important, and what's a distraction.

If a prospect uses it against you, ask to have separate meetings and allocate technical experts to work on each part of the deal. And if the documentation is too voluminous, ask specific questions and inquire on which exact part of the documentation the answer could be found.

Tactic 6: False concessions

False concessions are concessions that you place on the table to be taken by the other party. These are things you were not interested in to begin with, but you are putting them forward so you can give them away against something else in return. An example that is commonly cited comes from the workplace: An employee is asking for a salary increase and an extra paid holiday. The extra paid holiday is the false concession here. As the negotiation progresses, the employee would drop the holiday request and settle for the salary increase. What happened is that the employee gave away something he didn't want and didn't have to begin with, but obtained something that he really was interested in obtaining. One must be careful while using this tactic as it could back-fire. The employer could have agreed to offer the extra paid holiday but refuse to budge on the salary. Be prepared to respond to such scenario.

Now, one thing I want to clarify here about concessions before we move

互惠。当销售代表第一次见面就给出一份“免费提案”时，我就会提防。我问自己：“如果他们可以免费为我提供这些，那他们想从我这里得到什么样的回报呢？”唯一一个可以让步的例外是对方是你的长期合作伙伴，你们要么有很多利害关系，要么就是你们之间已经建立起了一种“双赢”的关系。

在你做出让步时：

- ■ 将其细分，不要直接给 10 个百分点的折扣，要先给 7 个，然后再给 3 个；
- ■ 要求对方给予回报，可以说：“我们已经对价格做了一些调整，我们希望你们现在也可以（加入请求问答）。”
- ■ 不要让你的让步显得非常容易，要让对方通过努力争取才能得到。

如果对方用这项策略对付你，你要如何回应？不幸的是，由于很难辨别对方事项的优先次序，你没有什么办法用以回应。一名谈判者通常会用一种

forward. In negotiation, concessions are **NOT given**, they are **TRADED**. You don't give them away unless you get something in return. It's called "Reciprocity." Every time a sales representative approaches me for the first time with a "free offer", my defenses go up. I ask myself "If they are giving this away for free, what are they expecting from me to reciprocate?" The only exception where you can make a concession, is when you are dealing with a long-term partner with whom there is so much at stake, or with whom you have established a "win-win" relationship mindset.

When you make the concession:

- Make them in small bits. Instead of discounting the price by 10, discount it first by 7, then by 3 afterwards.
- Ask for the other party to reciprocate by saying: "We have made some pricing adjustment. We expect that you are in a better position now to (insert request here). "
- Don't make it look like it was an easy concession to give away. Make the other party fight for it.

How to respond when this tactic is being used against you? Unfortunately,

很难分辨的方式来提要求，所以你很难猜到什么是对方在意的，什么又是对方不太在意的。你唯一能做的就是在谈判之前获得外部的信息，或者试着分析对方的肢体语言来寻求线索。

策略 7: 权限不足

这个策略经常会被对方作为一种力量来源使用。他们会故意给自己降权，目的是为了显示存在某种使他们无法达成一致意见的外部力量。有时候他们是真的没有权限，但有时不是。一个潜在客户可能会反复地对你使用这个策略，以此耗费你的精力，或者仅仅是作为一次性的策略来促使你做出退让。

事例：

买家：我们将会以 45 天为周期来付款。

卖家：我们的付款条约上是 30 天。

买家：我的权限只能同意 45 天付款。如果少于 45 天，我就需要去请示我们的 CFO。他现在正在度假，在两三周后才能回来。

卖家：我的权限也只能同意 30 天付款。不过既然这是成交前的最后一个问题，如果你可以在今天下单的话，我可以同意 45 天付款。我会在十月中旬安排与贵方的 CFO 会面，并在那时再作细节上的讨论。

在这段对话中，这个买家很聪明地宣称他们的决策者由于外出度假而无法联系。他之所以这么说是因为预测到该卖家可能会想要与他的 CFO 对话，而这便是他所能做的。如果对方要求更高的权限来推进交易，就得请求该“权力者”到场或马上通个电话。在打电话请示前先询问“贵公司是否需要某个人在场才能保证此次交易最终拍板”会比较保险。通过这个问题，你就能够发现谁是真正的决策者。

there is not much you can do because it is very hard to identify how the other party's priorities rank. A negotiator would usually make requests in a way that makes it difficult for you to guess what's more important to them and what's less. Your only bet here is to obtain outside information before the meeting or try to analyze body-language for clues.

Tactic 7: Limited Authority

This tactic is very commonly used by the other party as a source of strength. They would dis-empower themselves in purpose to indicate that there are external forces that don't allow them to reach a final agreement right there. Sometimes it is true, but some others it is not. A prospect might use this tactic repetitively against you to drain your energy, or use it as a one-time tactic to push you to back down.

Example:

Buyer: We will make payments by cycles of 45 days.

Seller: Our payment terms are 30 days.

Buyer: I only have authority to agree on the standard 45 days. If less, then I will need to check with our CFO on that. He is out on vacation but will return to office in two or three weeks.

Seller: I also have authority to agree only on 30 days payment terms. But since this is the last remaining point to close this deal, I can agree to a 45 days payment terms for this first order if you place it today. We will schedule a meeting with your CFO to meet mid–October and discuss it in detail.

In this dialogue, the buyer was smart enough to announce that the decision maker is out on vacation, hence can not be reached at the moment. He did this because he expects the seller to ask to talk to the CFO right there. And this is what is supposed to be done. If the other party invokes higher authorities to move forward,

如果你发觉你的谈话对象权限有限，并且在每次有新的提案时都要联系更高的权限者时，你可以采取以下措施。

■ 建议结束会议，重新安排一个决策者在场的新会议；

■ 用非对抗式的方式激发他们的个人意识，你可以这么说："我知道 × 先生的角色很重要，不过根据你过去的经验，他是否总是会接受你的建议呢？"

有时候，权限不够仅仅是一个幌子。对方只是用这个来争取更多的时间，或者以此把自己跟这个决策撇清关系。如果你想搞清楚，你可以问他，"如果您现在不得不自己做决定，您会达成这个交易吗？"如果他们说会，那么问他们在什么样的情况下他们能帮你达成这个交易；如果他们说不会，那么你可能需要停下来问更多的问题看看是什么妨碍了他们。

策略 8: 刻意曲解

对方假装对你的提案或意见疑惑不解，并以此来争取时间或设法发掘额外的信息。你可能会听到以下几种说话方式：

你可以重新向我解释一遍刚才的提案吗？

我不太理解你的报价；

我不确定自己有没有跟上你的节奏。

如果对方请求你做额外的解释，不要感到沮丧。有时候他们可能是真的没有明白。保持你的职业风范并控制好自己的情绪，然后重新向他们解释一遍你的想法。也许你开始的时候并没有解释清楚。

去年有个公司邀请我作为发言者参加他们公司的一次活动，电话那头的

either request to bring that "authority" to the table right there or give them a call right away. It is safe to start asking this question earlier on by inquiring if "anyone else from your side needs to be on board in order to OK this transaction". By asking that question, the real decision makers are uncovered.

If you detect that the party you are talking to has limited authority and invokes the higher authority every time a new proposal is made, you can either:

- Suggest stopping the meeting, and rescheduling a new one where the decision maker would be present.
- Appeal to their ego in a non-confrontational manner by saying something along these lines "I understand the input of Mr. X is important in such matters, but based on your past experience, would he often accept your recommendations?"

Sometimes the limited authority is just a bluff. The other party is using it to buy some more time, or absolve themselves from the responsibility to make a decision on the spot. If you detect that, you can ask the other party "If you had to make the decision right now, by yourself, would you agree to this deal as it is?" If they say yes then ask them what elements do they need to help them build a case for your offer. If they say no then you might need to step back and ask a few more questions to figure out what's holding them.

Tactic 8: Deliberate Misunderstanding

The other party pretends to be confused about a proposal or an agreement in order to buy time or extract additional information. A few versions of what you will hear:

Can you take me through that proposal again?

I'm having a hard time understanding your offer.

I'm not sure I'm following you here.

Don't be discouraged if the other party requests additional clarifications.

人紧接着向我讲解（讲解得很糟糕）各项事宜。我们在各个问题上徘徊不前，他一直说“不，不是，你不明白”，每次他这么说的时候，我都想回复他“你是在说我蠢吗？”

通常来说，在谈判或其他任何生活情境中，如果对方不明白，都是**你的问题**，而不是他们的。作为一名老练的销售代表，你必须知道如何将复杂晦涩的问题分解为通俗易懂的信息，并且不要在意一遍又一遍地向对方解释。

刻意曲解策略可以在谈判结束并且你已经同意了所有的条款后使用。有时你可以提交一份订单确认文件，而潜在客户在看到后则会说：“噢，我以为我提过 5 万美元的价格是 X 型号的，不是 Z 型号！目前我已经向我们的市场部确认过会投放广告，而且我们的财务部也已经准备好了资金。”

策略 9：退让

退让策略也称为**退避**策略。对谈判方的报价或还价表现出一种消极的反应来使他们对刚提过的要求感到忧虑。为达到更好的效果，常常将言语和非言语的表达混合使用。比如：

- 用表情和肢体动作表现震惊和意外；
- 明显的一次深呼吸；
- 摇头表示怀疑。

当你正确使用这些表达方式时，就会促使对方退让。

如果对方用这个策略对付你，坐等对方解释为何会有这样的反应。如果他

Sometimes they are genuinely confused. Stay professional and keep your emotions in check, then walk them through your idea again. Maybe you did not explain it clearly at the first place.

Last year I was contacted by a company to intervene as a guest speaker at one of their events, and the person on the phone proceeded to explain (poorly) the layout to me. As we were going back and forth in questions, he kept saying "No, no, you don't understand." Every time he used that statement, I was tempted to reply "Are you calling me stupid?"

As a general rule, in negotiation or in any other life situation, if the other party doesn't understand, it's **YOUR fault,** not theirs. As a skilled sales representative, you must know how to break down complex issues into understandable information, and don't hesitate to explain things over and over again.

The Deliberate Misunderstanding tactic could be used after the negotiation is over and you have agreed on everything. Sometimes you would submit an order confirmation document, and the prospect would look at it and say: "Oh, I thought we said 50,000 USD for the X model, not the Z model! I've already confirmed that to our Marketing Department so they can release the ads, and to our Finance Department to make the funds available".

Tactic9: The Flinch

It is also called **The Wince** tactic. It's a visible negative reaction to the other party's offer or counteroffer to make them feel uneasy with what they have just said. For a better effect, it is used as a combination of verbal and non-verbal language. It can be done by:

- Demonstrating shock and surprise on the face and with body-language.
- Taking a sharp intake of breath.
- Shaking the head in disbelief.

们没有解释，就对他们说，“你们似乎对我刚才说的话很震惊”，然后等待他们回答。

策略 10: 无策略

这是最简单也是最直接的一个策略，建议你仅在那些建立过商业合作关系的人身上使用。在这种情况下，你要通过公正合理的数字，以最好的方式展示报价，并告诉对方这是你能尽的最大努力。比如：“你可能认为应该从这个交易中获得更多，这合情合理。请允许我向你展示我们报价的具体构成以及为何是这样的价格。这个 ×× 材料的平均花费为每吨 ×× 元，每件 ×× 元，人工费是每小时 ×× 元，资金成本是 ×× 元。”一旦所有的细节都已经摊上了桌面，就可以告诉对方：“如果您能帮我们找到还有哪些地方可以减少花费，我们很乐意去做。”这个策略并不会百分之百有效，但是却可以帮你极大地加速销售流程。

既然它叫“无策略”，也就意味着没有谈判。你把你能提供的东西都摊上桌面，然后让你的合作伙伴用合理的判断与你共同推进交易。在你完成所有的陈述后，保持安静。

如果你只是采购了健身器械并将其安装在你的地下室里，是无法拥有傲人身材的，只有使用这些器械才行。现在你已经知道如何拿捏谈判技巧，我建议你从今天就开始尝试使用它们。

我目前正在将一些可以帮助公司提高谈判技巧的资源分享在我的博客中。（如果你想了解更多，请登录 www. eastheimer. com 这个网站）

When used properly, it could push the other party to back-down.

If used against you, just sit and wait for the other party to explain what made them react that way. If they don't, ask them by saying something like: "You seem surprised by what I have just said", and then let them talk.

Tactic 10: No Tactic

This is the simplest and most straightforward tactic to use. It is advised to use it only with parties with whom you already have an existing relationship. In this case you present your offer in the best light possible, with a justifiable number, and tell the other party that this is the best you can do. "You think you should get more out of this deal. That's legitimate. Let me show you how our offer is structured and how we reached that price. The … material costs an average of … per ton. That leaves us with a … per item. The cost of manpower is … per hour, and the cost of fund is ..." Once all the details are laid out, the end comes with "So if you can help me find any areas where we can reduce those numbers, we would be happy to do it". This tactic will not work 100% of the time, but will greatly help you accelerate the sales process.

Since it is called the "No Tactic", it calls for no negotiation. You put out there what you have to offer, and call on your partner's good judgment to proceed with the deal. When you finish your monologue, keep quiet.

Simply buying and installing exercising equipment in your basement doesn't lead to a good-looking body. Only the use of the equipment does. Now that you know how negotiations are to be handled, I suggest you go ahead and use what you have learned starting today.

I'm working on putting a blog up to share additional resources that could help companies improve their negotiation skills. (Head over to *www.eastheimer.com* for more.)

“我告诉过你不要将威胁当作一种谈判技巧。”

"I told you to stop using threats as a negotiation technique."
Abdelhak Benkerroum

| 第二部分 |

打造一支优秀的销售团队

如果你处在一个全球化的环境里，那你一定要多留个心眼。你的竞争者正夜以继日地争取市场份额，除非你已经有一个长远的计划并对销售流程有着全面的把控，否则来自国内外的竞争者就会追赶上你。这不是“他们是否会赶上你”的问题，而是“他们何时会赶上你”的问题。

销售流程并非是以辨识开始、以成交结束那么简单。它还应包括：1. 雇用正确的员工；2. 留住正确的员工；3. 评估销售人员。这正是我在这个部分要谈的内容，主要是针对那些正在努力培训他们的销售团队并走向成功的销售经理们。

这部分内容同时也适用于销售代表，可以让他们知道在面试一个职位的时候会出现哪些情况，如何评价他们自己的表现，如何对待他们的经理，当获得销售部门内部晋升后又该如何做。

| Part 2 |

Building an Outstanding Sales Team

If you live in a global environment, you have to be paranoid. Competitors work around the clock to gain market shares, and unless you have a long term vision and full control of your sales process, domestic and foreign competition will catch up with you. It's not a question of "if they will", it's a question of "when they will".

The sales process doesn't start with the prospection and end with closing the deal. It must include: 1. hiring the right people, 2. keeping the right people, 3. assessing the salespeople. This is what this part of the book will address. It is primarily directed to the sales managers who are struggling to put the right ingredients together for their sales team to succeed.

It is also directed to Sales Representatives. It will tell them what to expect when they go for a job interview, how to assess their own performance, what to expect from their managers, how to act when they get promoted to a higher position within their sales department.

如何挑选最适合的销售代表

在一个组织中，人力资源总监（CHO）无疑是继首席执行官（CEO）之后最重要的人。由于人力资源（HR）部门的工作很难被量化，许多公司都低估了它的作用。我们可以通过数据看到任意一名销售代表在某一个月创造的收益，也能通过数据知道某个客服人员处理了多少文件。但是对于 HR 专员，我们要通过哪些数据来衡量他们的表现？所以你会发现许多公司的 HR 部门同时也要负责组织年会、调排假期、计划生日派对等。这多么浪费他们的才能啊！你的 HR 经理或 HR 部门应该帮你雇用正确的员工，培训并评估他们，将他们安排到正确的职位上去。正确的职位安排与正确的员工雇用同样重要。拿一支足球队来说，如果教练交换了守门员和攻击型中场的位置会发生什么？毫无疑问会一片混乱。如果你把这些球员安排到错误的位置上去，他们无论多么出色，都无法发挥出应有水平。放到公司上也是一样的道理：应当谨慎挑选销售人员，并给予他们各种支持让他们发挥才干。

那么，在销售经理的帮助下，人力资源部门应当如何雇用正确的销售人员呢？

一名优秀的 HR 专员知道：

- 销售人员擅长推销产品，包括推销他们自己，即使他们并非你们公司的最佳选择；
- 某一销售人员在其他公司表现良好并不意味着他能够在你的公司做得同样出色。

一名优秀的 HR 专员还知道公司要想获得成功，它的每个职位的人员具体都需要什么样的技能和个性。这是关键，同时也是单独设立 HR 经理的原

Hiring the right people

The most important person in an organization after the CEO is undoubtedly the head of Human Resources (HR). Many companies underestimate the role of their HR department because its activity can not be easily quantified. We can look at the data and tell the revenue generated by any sales representative in a given month. We can also look at the data and tell how many files were handled by a customer service agent. But when it comes to HR, which data do we look at to measure their performance? So you will find many companies where the HR department is tasked with organizing end of year dinners, arranging vacations, scheduling birthday parties…What a waste of talent! Your HR manager or HR department should help you hire the right people, train them, evaluate them, and place them at the right positions. Placing employees at the right position is as important as hiring the right employees. Look at a soccer team and think of what would happen if the coach swaps the positions of the goalkeeper and the attacking midfielder. No doubt a mess will ensure. No matter how good those players are, if you place them at the wrong positions, they will not perform. The same applies to companies: A salesperson should be carefully chosen and given the tools to over-perform.

So, how can the Human Resources department, with the help of the Sales Manager, hire the right salespeople?

A good HR knows that:

- Salespeople are good at selling things, including selling themselves, even when they are not the perfect fit for your company.
- Just because a salesperson has done well at another company doesn't necessarily mean that they will do well at yours.

A good HR also knows exactly what skills and personalities predict success in any given position within your company. That is the key. That's what sets HR

因所在。

我在下方列出了可以用来物色理想销售代表的具体步骤。HR 专员都知道这些，因此其扮演的角色是公司成功的关键。每个步骤都很重要，它们都是获得成功的重要因素。

提示 1: 写一份工作描述

你的公司应该在潜在员工提问之前准备好一份单页的职位描述，上面写明新员工的各项职责以及需要达成的岗位目标。如果你是一名销售代表，当有一家公司联系你并表明想要雇用你，却没有告诉你明确的工作职责以及他们对工作表现的要求时，别理会他们。

提示 2: 内部寻找

你很难在外面找到出色的销售人员，因为出色的销售人员并不会放弃他们目前还不错的工作。在你到市场上到处发放“我们在招人”的广告前，销售经理和 HR 经理应该先看看那些现有的员工，并根据他们的个性、技能和聘期进行筛选，然后评定哪些人有可能加入销售团队。当你去开发现有资源的时候，你的投入会大大减少。

如果无法在内部找到潜力候选人，可以让公司里的员工推荐前职员或者他们在之前的工作中认识的合适人选。有些公司甚至会设立一个转介绍项目，任何员工推荐的人一经录用，推荐者都能够获得一笔奖金。

managers apart.

I'm listing the steps that will guide you in your hunt for the ideal sales representatives. An HR already knows that, hence its pivotal role in the company's success. No one step is more important than the other. They are all critical for your success.

Pointer 1: Write down a job description

Before the potential hire asks you for it, your company should be able to produce a one-page document that summarizes the duties of the new hire and what results they will be accountable for. If you are a sales representative and you get approached by a company that wants to hire you, but doesn't tell you exactly what will be your duties and what are their expectations in terms of performance, walk away.

Pointer 2: Look internally

Great salespeople will always be hard to find externally because great salespeople don't leave great jobs. Before going posting a "We Are Hiring" sign all over the marketplace, the sales and HR managers should take a look at their existing employees, and identify, based on character, skills, and tenure who might be approached with a proposition to join the sales team. The cost of hiring and training is a lot lower when you tap into existing resources.

If no potential candidate could be found internally, employees within the company can be asked to recommend ex-colleagues or people they know from their previous jobs. Some companies even put in place a referral program whereby a bonus is given to any employee who proposes a candidate that ends up being hired.

提示 3: 利用竞争者

来自竞争者的销售人员非常熟悉市场，如果他们在加入你公司的同时还能带来之前的客户资源就更理想了。找找看那些正在经历管理层变动的竞争者，他们往往会有人员上的调整，这给你足够的机会来探查优秀的人选并将他们吸引过来。

为防止与竞争者出现人才争夺战，HR 经理可以和外部的招聘代理公司合作，让它们充当这项事务的中间人。

提示 4: 评估自己公司的环境

如果你的公司没有市场和销售支持，那么那些曾在其他提供支持的公司表现突出的员工就会在你的公司黯然失色。你应该寻找那些来自结构和商业文化与你的公司比较相近的企业的求职者。一名来自跨国公司的销售人员习惯于被安排在有产品和市场支持的环境中工作。比如管理层陪同他参加客户会议，客户关系管理软件帮他组织和分析销售数据，行政助理为他安排日程等。如果把他安排在什么支持都没有的粗犷体系里，他可能不会待太久。

提示 5: 知道如何阅读简历

简历是营销材料，而且它也确实应该被这样看待。简历突显实力和成就，隐藏不足。一个明智的销售人员不会在简历上告诉你“我有 40% 的配额没有完成”。一名优秀的 HR 专员知道如何阅读简历。举个例子，如果有一名 B2B 销售代表在上一家公司的工作时间不足 6 个月，当你看到他的简历时就要注

Pointer 3: Tap into the competition

Salespeople coming from the competition will have a good understanding of the market, and would ideally join your company bringing with them an existing portfolio of customers. Look at competitors that are undergoing a management change, and it's likely that there will be movement within their teams, enough movement for you to detect good talent and attract them.

To prevent starting a talent war with the competition, the HR manager can work with an external hiring agency to be the middle-man in the transaction.

Pointer 4: Assess your own environment

If your company doesn't have a marketing support and sales support, then the candidate who did outstandingly in another supportive company will fail miserably in yours. You should look for candidates who come from structures and business cultures slightly similar to yours. A salesperson from a multinational is used to work in environment where product and marketing support his prospection, the management accompanies him to customer meetings, a Customer Relationship Management Software helps organizing and analyzing his sales data, an administrative assistant organizes his day… Put him in a small structure where none of the above exists, and he might not last long.

Pointer 5: Know how to read a CV

Resumes are marketing material and they should be treated as such. They highlight strengths and accomplishments but omit failures. No reasonable salesperson will tell you on their CV "I failed to make the quota by 40%". A good HR knows how to read a résumé. For example, if a B2B sales representative who has worked in his last company

意了。这是因为一名销售代表平均需要 3 个月的时间来适应一份新工作，并需要另外的3个月进入工作的最佳状态。如果他在之前公司只待了大约6个月，那可能就意味着他没有达标，不要录用他。我的朋友埃萨姆是一家美国跨国公司的销售总监，我曾问他是怎么看简历的。他说："简历本身并不能告诉我太多有关求职者的信息。我从简历中能获得的唯一有价值的信息就是他 / 她在一家公司里待了多少年。如果他 / 她在很多公司待的时间都很短，那我可能会觉得这个人只对快钱感兴趣，而没有职业前景规划，只要有人给他 / 她稍高点的薪水，他 / 她就会离开我的公司。奉献精神和责任感非常重要。"

提示 6: 将求职者视为你的客户

第一印象很重要。如今，吸引到出色的销售代表很难，所以，要及时地回复他们的电子邮件；如果他们来到你的办公室面试，要准时在接待室欢迎他们并亲自带他们到会议室；保持你办公室的整洁，肢体语言尽可能积极开放等。我总是在与某家公司交流之初，就开始观察这些重要的细节。你也不想让你的公司在市场上被视为一家"没有规矩的公司"吧？

提示 7: 学习如何主导一次面试

在面试一名潜在员工时，准备一份提问的问卷。当你客观地比较了两位求职者谁表现得更好，却还是无法决定该录用谁时，这份问卷就能在面试的最后阶段给你极大的帮助。查明他们是否清楚自己之前工作中的最小的细节方面的数字：上一份工作中每天拨打多少电话？完成了多少交易？创造了多少收益？在众多的问卷问题中，其中有五个问题是我每次都会问的，它们是：

for less than 6 months approaches you, it should raise a red flag. This is because it takes a new salesperson three months on average to learn a new job, and an extra three months to start working at full speed. If their jobs at their previous companies lasted only 6 months or so, it probably means they didn't make the numbers. Don't hire them. I asked my friend Essam, Director of Sales at a US multinational on what he looks for in a CV. He said that: "The CV doesn't tell me much about the candidate. The only valuable information I get from it is how many years he or she spent in a company. If he or she has worked in many companies within a short period of time, then I might think that this is not a person interested in a career path but rather in quick profit, a person who would leave my company as soon as someone else gives him a slightly higher salary. Dedication and commitment are very important in this function".

Pointer 6: Treat the candidate as your customers

First impressions matter. Good sales representatives are hard to come by nowadays. Respond to their emails on a timely manner. If they come to your office for an interview, be on time, welcome them at the reception and personally walk them to the meeting room, keep your office clean, and display open body-language. The list can go on and on. These are important details that I always look at as soon as I start interacting with a company. You don't want your company to be known around the marketplace as the "company that doesn't care", do you?

Pointer 7: Learn how to carry an interview

When interviewing a potential hire, come prepared with a questionnaire that lays out the questions you will be asking during the interview. That questionnaire will be of great help at the end of the process when you want to objectively compare two candidates who did well, but you still can't decide which one to hire. Find out if they know their numbers down to the smallest detail: How many calls they made

问题 1：“在过去的 6 个月中，你最骄傲的三件事是什么？”

这样我便可以知道他们是如何描述自己的成就的，以及他们是否会在谈论成就时赞扬团队中的其他成员。

问题 2：“请讲述你的一次失败的经历。”

通过这个问题我可以看出他们是否将学习视为该过程的一个部分，以及他们是否知道自己能在未来做出什么样的改变。

问题 3：“请告诉我你最不喜欢的同事是什么样的。”

如果他将回答简化为一个标签，比如说他称某个人是个骗子，这并非是个好迹象。那些愿意与人达成一致意见的人并不会用标签来评判事物，而是通过更为复杂的描述。

问题 4：“为什么我要录用你而不是其他人？”

通过这个问题可以判断他们的自信以及他们的说服能力。

问题 5：“你为什么辞掉上一份工作？”

我喜欢用这个问题来了解这个人不喜欢什么，以及他们识别自身错误的能力。

如果你是一名销售代表，那么你在前去面试时就要准备好回答这些问题。万一 HR 专员或销售经理没有问你这些刁钻的问题的话，你可以问他们！在你跳槽到一家刚刚有所了解的公司之前，问问他们具体对你有什么期望。

提示 8: 学习如何测试新雇员

3 个月之后，你应该就可以看出新录用的销售代表的业绩是好是坏了。要么好，要么不好，没有中间选项。在第一天，不是第二天也不是第三天，就要让新雇员制订出一份第一个月、第二个月、第三个月的计划，以此显示他们打算如何度过入职后的前几个月。这个计划可以让你了解新雇员的想法以

each day in their last job? How many deals did they close? How much revenue did they generate? Out of the many questions in the questionnaire, there are five questions I always make sure I ask, and those are:

QUESTION 1: "What are the three things you are proudest of from the past six months?"

Here I assess how they describe their achievement, and if they credit other team members when discussing achievements.

QUESTION 2: "Tell me about a failure."

Here I see if they acknowledge learning as part of the process, and if they are able to identify what they could change in the future.

QUESTION 3: "Tell me about your least preferred co-worker."

If they reduce their answer to a label such as saying that person is a liar, then it's a bad sign. People who are open to reach agreements don't judge using labels, but paint a more complex picture.

QUESTION 4: "Why should I hire you and not someone else?"

This question gauges their confidence as well as their ability to convince.

QUESTION 5: "Why did you leave your last job?"

I like to ask this question to understand what does the candidate not like, and eventually their ability to recognize their mistakes.

If you are a sales representative going to such interviews, be prepared to answer those questions. In case the HR or Sales manager doesn't ask you those tough questions, you can ask them! Before jumping into a company you have just met, ask what exactly is expected from you.

Pointer 8: Learn how to test new hires

After 3 months on the job, you should be able to look at the newly hired sales representative's numbers and either be impressed or depressed. Nothing in between. On the first day, not the second nor the third, on the first, ask the new hire to work

及他将如何组织想法并付诸行动，使其转化为公司的收益以及他自己的佣金。如果他们无法完成自己制订的计划，那你就知道该怎么做了。成功的企业雇人很慢，解雇很快。你可以指引他们去那些他们有机会获得成功的公司，这样也是帮助他们了。

没有哪个销售经理或者 HR 经理能说自己从未在职业生涯中犯过雇用团队成员的错误。有些错误的代价比其他错误的高很多。在一些高度工会化的行业里解雇一个人是极为困难的，所以你最终会因为雇用了一个不好的人而拖累整个团队。你只能选择试着将他们安排在其他的部门，看看他们是否在其他地方彰显价值，或者你只能等着他们自己打包走人。

这些提示虽然不能保证你可以雇用到最好的人，但是却可以帮你将失败的风险降到最低。

如果你是一名刚被录用的销售代表，当你第一天走进办公室的时候，发现公司已经为你准备好了电话，装配好了电脑，甚至连你的名片都已经印刷出来，那么你大概是来到了一家不错的公司。这些都显示出他们在商业组织上的专业风范。而这是一个绝佳的迹象，后面我们还会揭示企业留人的一些其他方法。

on a 1-month, 2-month, and 3-month plan to show you how they will spend the first months on the job. That plan will give you an idea on how the new hire thinks, and how he can organize those thoughts and put them into action that translates into revenue for your company, and commissions for him. If they fail to deliver on a plan they themselves wrote, then you know what you have to do. Successful companies hire slowly, but fire quickly. You will do that candidate good by directing them to other companies where they can succeed.

No sales manager or HR manager could claim they have never made a mistake sometimes during their career by hiring the wrong team-member. Some mistakes are more costly than others. In some highly unionized industries, it is extremely difficult to fire a person, so you end up with a bad hire who is a burden on the team. You're left with the choice of exploring the possibility of placing them in another department to see if they can perform in other areas, or wait for the moment they will pack and leave.

These tips do not guarantee you will have the best hire either, but will help you minimize your risks of failure.

If you are a newly hired sales representative, and you walk into your office the first day, and your cell-phone is ready, your laptop is already configured, and your business cards have been printed, then you have probably landed in a good company. It shows you that they are professional in their approach to business. That's a great first sign. Let's find out about the other good signs.

留住人才的 7 种方式

我在前面谈到过应当将新员工视为新客户来对待。客户是有价值并应以礼相待的。如果是好客户，我们就应该竭尽所能来防止他们落入竞争者的手中。

以下便是留住优秀销售人员的方法。

提示 1: 经济上的奖励

想象一下如果你的小孩每次在屋子里打破某样东西，他 / 她都可以拿到一颗糖果，那将会发生什么？为了得到更多的糖果，小孩会继续损坏东西。无论在生活中，还是在商业上都是如此，一个人因为**奖励养成了自己的行为习惯**。一名超额完成任务、表现出色的销售代表也应当获得额外的回报，最理想的形式就是每月的固定薪资再加上占利润一定百分比的可变薪资。是利

Retaining the right people

I said in the previous pages that a new candidate should be treated as if he was a new customer. Customers are valued and treated with respect. When they are good customers, we should do everything in our power to prevent them from throwing themselves into the competition's arms.

Here is how to keep good salespeople.

Pointer 1: Financial rewards

Imagine if every time your kid breaks something in the house, he or she is handed a candy. Guess what would happen? In order to score more candies, the kid will keep breaking things around. In life as in business, **you get the behavior you reward**. A sales representative who over-delivers and does an exceptional job should get an exceptional pay check, ideally made of a fixed monthly salary, and a variable commission representing a percentage of the profit. A percentage of the

润的百分比（收入减去开支），而非收入的百分比。如果销售人员的酬劳是按收入百分比来算的，那即使是不盈利的交易他们也能获得报酬，我想你是不会希望出现这种情况的。

提示 2: 个人认可

每个人都喜欢被认可，特别是高成就者。如果你的公司还没有诸如“年度销售明星”“年度之星”或者其他类似的奖项的话，现在是时候去设立了。这一举措几乎不需要任何成本，但却可以让公司里的每个人都知道，所有人的工作表现和才能都是被认可的。我曾看到一些公司前台的墙上挂着颜色醒目、题为“最佳销售员”的牌匾，上面有员工的名字、照片和赞语。最佳销售员还会得到一个奖杯，他们可以把它放到自己的客厅，获得来自家人和朋友的赞赏。最终他们还将带回家一张支票。但是认可不应该仅限于此，要让奖赏员工成为销售部门的一个习惯。举办惊喜派对，邀请团队成员共进晚餐，组织周末外出活动，无论市场境况如何都不吝一同举杯欢庆。这些都能够振奋销售人员并促使他们越战越勇。

提示 3: 培训与个人发展

这一条非常重要。好公司雇用优秀人才，并将他们打造得更为出色。无论一名销售代表有多优秀，都还是有提升的空间的。有些公司只培训他们的员工如何保持好的卫生和生活方式，比如说阿迪达斯（Adidas），这家公司无偿为员工提供免费的健康检查，来帮他们查验会影响生产率的潜在或已有的健康问题，比如说血压或背部问题。然后这些员工会得到来自专业健康顾问

profit (revenue minus cost), not a percentage of the revenue. If the salesperson's pay is based on revenue, then they will be rewarded even on unprofitable sales, and you don't want that to happen.

Pointer 2: Personal recognition

Everyone likes recognition, especially high achievers. If your company doesn't have awards such as "Salesperson of the Year" or "Star of the Year" or something similar, it's time to set that up. It costs close to nothing but these demonstrate to everyone that in your company, performance and talents are recognized. I have walked into companies where the reception's wall displayed in high colors a "Top Sales Performer" plaque with name and picture and words of praise. The top performer also takes home a trophy they can display in their living room for family and friends to see and acknowledge. They eventually take home a check too. But recognition should not be limited to that. Make employee appreciation and recognition a habit within your Sales department. Throw surprise parties, invite the team to dinners, go on week-end outings, toast successes and celebrate milestones regardless of the business climate. These will re-energize the salespeople and push them to aim for more.

Pointer 3: Coaching and personal development

This one ranks very high on the list. Good companies hire good people and build them into better ones. No matter how good a sales representative is, there is always room for improvement. Some companies go as far as coaching their employees on how to maintain a good hygiene and life style. So is the case of Adidas for example. The company organizes voluntary free health checks for its employees to help them identify any potential or existing health issues that will affect their productivity such as blood pressure or back problem. Then the

的指导，内容包括如何锻炼、如何健康饮食，以保持体型并在工作中表现出最佳水平。

提示 4: 赋权

最好的经理与你探讨项目，不会详细谈论他们自己的办事细则。他们会赋予你足够的自由去选择自己的方法来解决问题并达到目标。然后他们会说："嘿，需要帮忙的话尽管来找我。"

销售代表必须被赋予做困难决定的权力，而不是让销售经理像照看小孩一样每天监督着他们。如果你因信任而雇用了某个员工，那么是时候通过相信他们能够根据自己的出色判断力和能力做决定，来表现你的信任。当他们去与潜在客户会面时，他们应该获得公司在这方面的指导，并被赋予当场作出最终决定的权力，比如承诺某事或者完成交易。

提示 5: 公平

销售代表需要借助工具来充分发挥才能，并且团队中的每个销售代表都应该得到相同的工具。佣金和奖金方案要明确且对每个人都公平。公司里的其他职能比如说营销和客户服务需要对所有的销售团队成员提供公正、无偏颇的支持，因为偏颇会扼杀集体的团结。

你需要让你的员工和你站在同一战线，特别是在经济困难时期。如果你公正地对待他们，他们也必定不会辜负于你。

employees are given advice and guidance by professional health advisors on how to exercise and eat healthy in order to stay in shape and perform well at work.

Pointer 4: Empowerment

The best managers discuss projects with you, without discussing their implementation down to the smallest details . They give you enough freedom to choose your own approach to solve problems and reach goals. They then make themselves available with a "Hey, let me know if you need my help."

Sales representatives must be empowered to make tough decisions by themselves, without the sales manager having to babysit everybody on a daily basis. If you trusted someone by hiring him, it's time to show your trust by trusting their good judgment and ability to decide. When they go to meet with prospects, they should be aware of the company's guidelines in that regard, and be empowered to call shots right there on the spot, being it committing to something or closing a deal.

Pointer 5: Fairness

A sales representative needs tools to perform, and he should get the same tools as his other colleagues within the team. The commission or bonus scheme should be clear and fair for everyone. The other functions of the company such as marketing and customer service will have to provide support to all the sales team members without favoritism, because favoritism kills the morale of the group.

You need your people to stick with you, especially in times of economic difficulties. When you are fair with them, they certainly will be fair with you.

提示 6: 包容失败

犯错、失策和判断失误都是学习的机会，同时也都是这场游戏的一部分。没有谁能说自己从未在职业生涯中犯过错。

要给销售代表一些犯错和知错的空间，只要不让犯错成为一种习惯，只要没有给公司造成尽大的伤害，犯错就不算是件坏事。如果一名销售代表犯错了，这也说明他正在尝试着去做某事。那些什么都不去尝试的人当然不会犯错，而他们没法取得成功也不足为奇。

提示 7: 愿景

在构建一所房子前，建筑师会事先做好全方位的细节规划。如果建造者没有在开工前就将房子的最终效果图装在脑袋里，那么这个房子是不可能建成的。在商业上也是一样，管理层需要尽可能清楚地告诉员工公司的短期和长期发展目标是什么。这样一来，就没有人再在公司里琢磨自己该做什么了。每个人都将会有自己的奋斗目标和衡量自身价值的指标。

常会有团队成员问这样的问题："我该如何规划未来的这三年？"当公司里的每个人都各司其职时，这就不是什么难题了。那些帮助员工制定 5 年和 10 年规划的公司，通常都会严肃对待员工的长期愿景。

Pointer 6: Tolerance for failure

Mistakes, missteps, and incorrect judgments are all learning opportunities, and they are part of the game. No one can claim that they have never made a mistake in their career.

Leave room for the sales representatives to fail and learn from their failures. Failure is good, as long as it doesn’t become a habit, and as long as it doesn’t hurt the company at massive scales. If a sales representative is failing, it means that he is out there trying things. Those who don’t try anything are the ones who never fail. Not surprisingly, they are also the ones who never win.

Pointer 7: Vision

Before a house is built, the architect lays down the exact plan of the house, down to the smallest details. No house can rise and sustain itself if the builders do not have in mind the end result before they even start. The same applies to businesses. Management needs to tell its employees in the clearest way possible what are the short and long term growth goals of the company. By doing so, no one will be hanging around the company wondering what is expected of them. Everyone will have goals towards which they are striving and metrics against which they are assessed and held accountable.

It is normal for a team member to ask questions such as: “Where should I see myself 3 years from now?” When everyone in the company is accountable, answers to this question become easy. Companies that help their employees develop a 5-year plan and 10-year plan are generally companies that are serious about their long term vision.

使用正确的方法考核员工

在销售中，我们只能提高那些可以衡量的指标。我希望所有参与销售的人每天都能够重复一遍这句话。我坚信评估和考核的作用，因为它们可以告诉我们什么有用，什么没用，还有最重要的一点——为什么。

假如你是一位销售经理，你走向一位销售代表，告诉他由于他的业绩不太令人满意所以公司不再需要他。他将会问你的第一个问题是："你是怎么得出我的表现不令人满意这样的结论的？"如果你回答说他带来的收入比预期目标要少，那么你就是一个可能错误地开除了一名优秀销售员的坏经理。你该进行反思了。如果是和他商谈的客户在下单前还需要一些时间考虑呢？如果是他带来的那些客户产生了 30% 的利润率，而他的同事持续地带来类似的客户创造了很高的收入，但利润极低呢？还有那些他为高管准备紧急销售报告的周末夜晚呢？

Assessing sales representatives

In sales, we can only improve what we measure. I wish everyone involved in sales repeated that to himself every day. I strongly believe in evaluation and assessments because they tell us what's working, what's not, and most importantly, why.

Imagine you are a sales manager, and you walk up to one of your sales representatives and let him know that he will need to leave the company because his performance is not satisfactory. The first question he will ask you is: "How did you come to the conclusion that my results are not satisfactory?" If you answer that the revenue he generated was below the target, then you are a bad manager who is probably firing a good salesperson. Shame on you. How about the customers he negotiated with but they still need some time to think before placing an order? How about those customers with whom he made a 30% margin, whereas his colleagues keep bringing similar customers, but each with high revenue, yet extremely low profit? How about the Sunday nights he spent preparing those urgent sales reports for the top management?

我的意思是你应该用全面的体系来评估你整个团队的表现并做出判断。销售代表会从公正的业绩评估中获益良多，而要想公正，就需要全面评估。这是因为大多数人形成的观念和想法并不总是与员工销售行为的实际情况相匹配。数字不会说谎，本着公正的精神，销售经理应当根据态度、资质和交付能力设立明确的指标来对每一位销售代表进行评估和判断。

这意味着什么？

这意味着每个销售代表都应该与其直属经理每月进行一次例会，从两个方面探讨自己的业绩表现：量化指标和行为表现。是月度会议，而非年度会议。如果等到年底再来评估销售团队的表现，那我们就会错过 11 个月的潜在成长机会。记住，可以衡量的工作才能去完成。

当然，这些月度会议也不应该影响到你与团队的广泛交流，无论是在个人还是团队层面。你可以在与业内销售代表的交流中学到很多东西，并见证他们是如何开展工作的。

现在我们就分别来看看这些评估指标吧。

提示 1：量化指标

量化指标是由硬数据组成的，所以很容易收集。数据反映事实，由于商业性质和销售渠道的不同，不同行业间的指标会有很大的差距。根据我的经验，我建议使用 5 到 6 个指标。太多会造成混乱，太少不够全面，都不足以达到预期目标。例如：

- 销售收入，指销售产品的总收入；
- 利润，收入减去成本，销售代表应该有一个按销售收入百分比计算的

My point is that the picture should be complete in order for you to assess the performance of your team and make a judgment. Sales representatives benefit greatly from objective assessment of their performance, and in order for it to be objective, it needs to be complete. That is because most people develop concepts and ideas that do not always match the real picture of how well (or how bad) employees are doing in their sales activity. Numbers do not lie. In the spirit of fairness, sales managers should set clear metrics to judge and evaluate every single sales representative based on attitude, aptitude, and ability to deliver.

What does this mean in clear terms?

It means that every sales representative should have a monthly meeting with his direct manager to discuss his performance on two categories: quantitative, and behavioral. Monthly meetings, not yearly meetings. If we wait until the end of the year to measure objectively how our sales team is doing, then we have just missed 11 months of potential growth. Remember, what gets measured gets done.

Of course, these monthly meetings should not prevent you from having extensive interactions with the team on an individual and group level. You learn a lot by going with the sales representatives on the field and witnessing how they go about their days.

Let's look into each one of those categories separately.

Pointer 1: Quantitative

This is hard data that is easily collected because it consists of numbers. And data speaks. The indicators vary greatly from industry to industry depending on the nature of the business and the sales channels. Based on my experience, I recommend to have 5 or 6 indicators. Too many will create confusion and too few will not give the exact picture we are trying to get to. An example of those indicators:

■ Sales revenue. The gross income received from the sale of the product.

■ Profit. The revenue minus cost. Sales representatives should have a target

目标利润；

- ■ 面对面会谈或者销售电话的数量；
- ■ 带来的新客户数量；
- ■ 客户的最新成交数量，以及老客户的新订单成交数量。

提示 2: 行为表现

无论销售代表在量化指标方面有多出色，他们对工作或者客户的态度，都要纳入考量。虽然是主观指标，但有些还是可以通过 1 到 10 的数字等级来相对客观地进行评价，“1”表示最差，“10”代表最好。再重申一次，没有必要使用很多指标，5 到 6 个就足够了。以下是评估行为表现的一个例子，也是我比较喜欢用的一些指标：

- ■ 及时性，该员工做事的时效性怎么样？他总能准时上班吗？他准时提交报告吗？他及时回复邮件和电话吗？
- ■ 对内部的态度，团队里的其他人怎么看待他？该名员工是否与同事相互尊重？
- ■ 对外界的态度，该名员工会花时间培养客户关系吗？客户具体又是如何看待他的？
- ■ 信守公司文化，该名员工遵守公司规章制度吗？他遵从并执行公司管理层的策略吗？
- ■ 自我发展，从上一次的评估到现在，该名员工产品和市场方面的知识有所增长吗？他接受了多长时间的培训？

一个月的周期很难看出行为表现上的改变，因此我建议一个月做一次量

profit by percentage of sales.

- Number of face to face meetings or calls placed.
- Number of new customers acquired.
- Number of deals closed with customers newly acquired and number of new deals closed with existing customers.

Pointer 2: Behavioral

No matter how good the sales representative does on the quantitative side, if they are displaying the wrong attitude at work or with customers, they should be held accountable. These are subjective metrics, but some objectivity can be built into them by ranking them on a scale from 1 to 10, where "1" is the least favorable outcome and "10" is the most favorable one. Here again, there is no need to have dozens of indicators. Just 5 ~ 6 indicators will be enough. An example of indicators that I like using to assess behavior:

- Timeliness. How timely the person is in his dealings? Does he always show up to work on time? Does he submit his reports on time? Does he answer emails and return calls on time?
- Attitude internally. How does the rest of the team view that person? Is this employee respectful in their interaction with the other employees?
- Attitude externally. Does this employee take time to nurture the relationship with the customer? How does the customer view this employee specifically?
- Adherence to the culture. Does this employee abide by the company's rules and guidelines? Does he follow and execute on the management's strategy for the company?

- Self-development. From the last assessment to this one, did the employee increase his knowledge of the product and the market? How many hours of

化指标的评估，每隔 3 或 6 个月进行一次行为表现的评估。

在明确这些指标后，逐一对应评估目标，从而确保每位销售代表都能达成这些指标。再次提醒，这都与每家公司的商业性质有关。对于一名物流公司的销售代表来说，每天与 3 位潜在客户进行 3 次不同的会谈是一个合理的目标，但如果是游艇销售员的话，就另当别论了。

我一般都会让销售代表自己设立目标，因为他们在这个行业已经有些时日了，明白什么样的目标可以实现，什么样的无法实现。然后我会拿他们提交的目标数字与上年的进行比较。接着，我再将这两者中较高的那一个作为该名员工的初始标准，并以特定的百分比每隔 3 个月进行一次提升。这样一来，目标既不会高得不现实，也不会低到影响我的商业成长。当然，3 个月后制定新目标的时候，会将当前的市场趋势以及客户的偏好都列入考量。这些目标和大体上的指标同时也会随着销售团队暴露出的弱点而改变。

这些目标不应该被用作惩罚销售代表的参考。相反的，它们应该以一种

training did he take?

It is difficult to see changes on behavioral results over a one-month period. So it is often suggested to carry a quantitative assessment every month, and a behavioral assessment every 3 or 6 months.

Once these measurements are identified, targets need to be put in place to insure every sales representative delivers on those measurements. Here again, it

will depend on the nature of the business the company is in. Having three meetings per day with three different prospects could be a reasonable target for a sales representative in a logistics company, but not reasonable for someone selling yachts.

What I generally do is to ask the sales representative to set those targets himself since he has been on the field for some time and knows what can be achieved and what can not. Then I take the numbers he proposed and compare them to the numbers from the previous year. I then take the highest one of the two and set it as a starting standard that will be increased by a specific percentage every three months. That way the targets are not too high to be unrealistic, nor too low to hurt the growth of our business. Of course, current market trends and customers' preferences are taken into account when

公正的方式用来帮助考量谁达标了，谁超额完成了，以及谁没有达到标准。而这也能够为每位销售人员提供足够的参照来认清自己在管理层支持、培训以及指导方面的需求。

评估过后，这四类员工会突显出来。

1. 杰出的销售人员。

这些员工是持续表现出色的销售明星。他们超额完成任务并几乎在每个指标上都超过了预期。他们应该当众获得褒奖并获得丰厚的回报。这么做可以给团队中的其他成员传递出一个强烈的讯号："我们重视表现超群的人，我们用奖杯和现金来表示对他们所付出努力的认可。现在你们面临的挑战便是成为像他们一样的人，那时我们也会用同样的方式奖励你们。"如果有晋升机会的话，这些人会被优先考虑。

2. 良好的销售人员。

他们是几乎总能达到配额目标的员工。虽有些许的失误，但他们在公司的标准下依然有着不错的稳定表现。他们太需要得到褒奖和奖励了。为促进他们拼搏上进并达到杰出的水平，应当对他们设立更高的门槛。同时他们也需要持续专注于个人发展并通过增强自身技能来实现进一步的提升。

3. 边缘销售人员。

这些员工会在月底的时候交付还过得去的业绩，但低于给他们设定的目标。如果他们的行为表现不错，但离优秀的量化指标还有些距离，那么他们就需要直属经理对其进行全面的培训和指导，并由他们的经理来决定他们是否还值得进一步的培训投资。一名优秀的经理会在这方面的管控上找到正确的平衡点，让员工从中学习、适应和成长，在此过程中不会让员工感到不受信任或缺乏信心。

new targets are being discussed three months later. Those targets, and the metrics in general, will also change once soft spots are discovered by the sales team.

These targets should not be used as a reference to punish sales representatives. Instead, they should help identifying, in a fair manner, who met, who exceeded, and who failed to meet the goals agreed on. And that will give each salesperson enough visibility to identify their needs in terms of management support, training, and coaching.

After the assessment, four categories of employees will stand out.

1. Outstanding salespeople.

These are the stars who outperform continuously. They exceed their quotas and over-deliver by almost every standard. These should be praised in public, and compensated generously. By doing so, a strong message is sent to the rest of the team that says "We value high performers, and we demonstrate it by recognizing their effort with trophies and with cash. Now your challenge is to be like them, and we will treat you like them." If there is a promotion in perspective, these are the first to be considered.

2. Good salespeople.

These are the team members who reached the targets assigned to them almost all the time. They stumbled a few times but their performance is still solid by company's standards. These are too eager to be praised and rewarded. The bar should be pushed higher to push them to strive and reach the outstanding level. They need to keep working on their personal development and building up their skills to move to the next step.

3. Marginal salespeople.

These deliver some OK results by the end of the month, but stay below the targets assigned to them. If they have demonstrated good behavioral results but less than good quantitative results, then they need extensive training and coaching from their direct manager. It's up to the manager to decide if they are worth the investment in training and coaching. A good manager will find the right balance in exerting enough control over those so they learn, adapt and grow, all without making it look like a lack of trust or confidence.

4. 不合格的销售人员。

有时也称其为“表现糟糕者”，不过我喜欢直接称其为“不合格的销售人员”。他们从没达到过自己的目标，并时常表现出满不在乎的态度。他们没有显露出任何前进或接受挑战的意愿。仅仅是和他们在一起，周围的同事就会感到没有动力，甚至心烦意乱。

赶快开除这样的员工吧！你开始的时候为何要雇用这些人？我不是在讲那些因为正经历着某些家庭困难而影响业绩表现的员工，那些人需要一些来自团队和经理的支持。我说的是那些从没为公司做过任何益事的员工。或许他们是碰巧走进了销售行业，那么现在他们需要离开了。

4. Bad salespeople.

Some call these “poor performers”, but I like to call them what they are “bad salespeople”. They never reach their targets and show up in the morning with that I-don’t-care attitude. They don’t display any willingness to move forward or take on challenges. Their colleagues feel demotivated or even frustrated just by having them around. Get rid of them. Why did you even hire them in the first place? I’m not talking here about employees going through hardship because of some family problems that’s affecting their results. Those ones need support from their team and from their manager. I’m talking about those employees who have not been doing any good for the company month after month after month. Maybe they ended up in sales by accident and they need to move on.

通过内部培训让销售代表适应外部变化

CFO：如果我们培训了员工而他们离开了怎么办?

CEO：如果我们没有培训员工而他们留下了怎么办?

以上的短对话广泛流传于世界各地的培训公司。它表现了某位停留于20世纪的CFO与一位21世纪的CEO之间的冲突。想象一下当有位医生告诉你："自从15年前毕业，我就再没有看过书也从未参加过医学研讨会。"那你还会信任这名医生吗？可能不会了吧。因为这15年来不断有新的技术引入医疗领域，也有新的病毒和疾病被发现，同时还有新的药物在获得专利后投入了市场。因此，单凭经验是不能定位一个人的声望的，不管是在医疗保健领域还是在其他任何领域。

如今的市场瞬息万变，而这些变化又往往是由那些很难左右的外部因素引起的。可能是新法规的出台，客户口味的改变，或者是新的竞争者的出现等，一支优秀的销售团队一定知道如何来应对这些变化。企业需要适应变化，而不是拒绝改变。其中一种方法便是在对员工的培训上做投资，并在公司内部培养人才，特别是销售人才，因为他们通常是非常注重职业生涯规划的，并且会勇于接受每一个挑战以提升他们自身的职业发展。

提示1: 认知内容

认知内容在很大程度上依赖销售代表的资历以及过去的销售经历。

如果是新雇用的销售代表，他需要在起初的几周跟着客户服务团队一起工作，客服人员最清楚公司为什么样的客户服务，他们的需求是什么，要面

Employee training

CFO: What if we train our employees and they leave?

CEO: What if we don't train them and they stay?

The above short exchange has been circulated widely among training companies around the world. It shows the contrast between someone stuck in the 20th century (CFO), and someone living in the 21st century (CEO). Imagine a doctor telling you "I have not read a book nor participated in a medicine seminar since I graduated 15 years ago." Would you still trust that doctor with your health? Maybe not. And that's because new technologies are constantly introduced to his field, new viruses and diseases are being discovered, new drugs are being patented and released to the market. So, experience alone does not define one's stature, being it in the healthcare field or any other field.

Today's markets change in an incredibly fast pace, and those changes are provoked by external parties that are not easy to tamper with. Being it the introduction of new laws, the change in customers' tastes, or the emergence of new competitors, a good sales force must know how to navigate those waters. Instead of resisting those changes, businesses need to adapt. One way to do so is to invest in coaching and developing talent within the company, especially salespeople, because they are generally very career focused, and will take up every battle to advance their careers.

Pointer 1: Content

The content depends greatly on the seniority of the sales representative and his past experience in sales.

If it's a newly hired sales representative, he will need to sit down with the customer service team for the first few weeks. Customer service people know exactly what kind of customers the company serves, their needs, the challenges

对什么样的问题，以及如何处理这些问题。让新人接一些电话或回复客服代表的电子邮件，这样他会更进一步了解客户以及公司的产品或服务。

等他们建立了自信，就可以将他们调回销售部门，同时安排更有经验的销售代表来指导他们。我曾在一家设有完善的“导师项目”的公司工作过，该项目根据每个新雇员的个性和所需的技能分别为其匹配一名公司的老员工作为指导。

我之前提到过，应该将刚开始的90天作为入职期。对于新销售代表所能带来的收入，预期应该接近于0，这很正常。你应该将焦点放在对他们进行广泛的培训以及为他们入职3个月之后深入市场做准备上。

如果某位销售代表已经入职有些时日了，那么有很多内容都可以对他进行辅导和培训。例如：

- 公司内部流程；
- 行业与市场信息；
- 肢体语言分析；
- 新产品或服务信息；
- 销售与谈判策略；
- 有效的沟通技巧；
- 潜在客户需求辨析。

你可以回到本书的第一部分，我在那里对谈判的步骤和流程都进行了探讨。销售流程的每一个阶段都可以作为一项不同的新培训，这是因为它们都是销售的基本要素。我曾经仅仅为了阐明“准备”这一阶段就花了一整天的时间，而且我可以告诉你的是，单是学习如何准备一次销售会议、辨识客户的真正需求或是完成一次交易，就有太多需要销售代表学习的东西。

they are facing, and how to address them. Let the new hire take some phone calls or respond to emails received by customer service representatives. He will get to learn more about the customer and the company's products or services.

Once they start gaining confidence, it's time to move them over to the sales department, and pair them with a more experienced sales representative. I have worked with companies that have in place a well established "Mentor Program", that's intended to match every new hire with a veteran of the company depending on personalities and skills needed to perform.

As I mentioned previously, the first 90 days should be considered as the onboarding period. The expectations from the new sales representative in terms of revenue generated should be close to 0. That is normal. The focus should be put on extensive trainings and preparation to go to the market 3 months after being hired.

If the sales representative has been with the company for some time, there is a lot he can be coached and trained on. A few examples would be:

- Internal company processes.
- Industry and market information.
- Body-language analysis.
- New product or service information.
- Sales and negotiation techniques.
- Effective communication skills.
- Prospect's needs identification.

You can go back to the first part of this book where I discussed the different steps of a negotiation, and take a look at the different parts of the process. Each phase of the sales process could be part of a new different training because those are the basics of selling. I was approached in the past to develop a full day training just to tackle the "Preparation" phase, and I can tell you that there are so many things a sales representative can learn just about preparing for a sales meeting, identifying the real needs of the customer, or closing a deal.

提示 2: 合理安排时间节点

辅导是一项随着商业行为推进而持续进行的活动。它应该是销售经理DNA 的一部分。与团队建立牢固而又深远的关系也是辅导的一部分。与出现失误的销售代表进行一次建设性的交谈是一种辅导，指导一名销售代表如何处理特定的情况也是一种辅导。也就是说，辅导有多种形式，无须在每周或是每月固定进行。

然而，如果是培训的话，应该根据产品和潜在客户的复杂性对员工设定参加培训时长的最低限额。平均每月 4 到 5 个小时是个不错的选择。就像之前提过的，新雇员的情况有所不同，他们需要在开始的 3 个月接受每天的培训。成功的经理会与他的团队和 HR 专员一起为员工规划他们未来 1 年、3 年以及 5 年的个人发展。经理帮助设计，员工来执行，HR 专员则确保其如期完

Pointer 2: A well worked out schedule

Coaching is an ongoing activity that occurs as events unfold. It should be part of the Sales Manager's DNA. Building strong and meaningful relationships with the team is part of the coaching. Having a constructive exchange with the sales representative who failed is a form of coaching. Teaching a sales representative how to handle a specific situation is a coaching. That is to say, coaching can take different forms, and doesn't need to be formalized by a weekly or monthly meeting.

However, when it comes to training, a minimum quota should be required from employees depending on the complexity of the product and the complexity of the prospects. An average of 4 to 5 hours of training per month is a good amount of time to spend on training. This doesn't apply to the new hires because as we saw earlier, they will need a daily training for their first 3 months. Successful managers sit down with their team along with their human resources representative to draft a 1-year, 3-year, and 5-year personal

成。这样一来，销售人员就能清楚地看到公司对自己的用心投资，而这便是员工留下来的理由。

最好的培训时间是在一年中商业活动不太频繁的时候，这不仅可以保持销售代表的参与度，也能防止他们失去动力或积极性（或两者都丧失）。

提示 3: 如何进行培训

在你决定如何对销售团队进行某一方面的培训前，最好先想想这几个问题：

- 这是对团队的全新培训还是一种强化和进修？
- 这是针对团队所有人的还是针对特定的一些人的？
- 希望这个培训解决什么样的具体问题？为什么需要以这样的培训作为开始？
- 就时间和金钱而言，应该投入多少用于这个培训？

你也不妨听听销售代表的意见，比如简单地问："你觉得怎么样更好呢？"

一旦回答完这些问题，公司就可以决定如何进行培训了，同时也可以选择是采用内部培训还是外包培训。

1. 内部培训。

可以由 HR 经理与销售经理合作安排培训。就资金而言，这样的培训成本不高，但是操作起来很费时间。其好处是这样的培训是由内部人员根据公司具体情况和面对的挑战量身定制的。一个比较好的例子是宜家每年都会进行的"'反官僚'作风活动周（anti-bureaucratic week）"。在这一周时间里，所有的经理都必须穿上售货员的制服，然后做所有的基层工作，比如操作收银

development plan for their employees. The manager helps design it, the employee implements it, and the HR makes sure it gets done. Done this way, the salesperson can see clearly how the company is investing in him or her. And that makes employees stay.

The best time to deliver training is during the time of the year where commercial activity slows down. It will keep the sales representatives engaged and prevent them from losing momentum or motivation (or both).

Pointer 3: How to deliver training

Before deciding on how to go about the trainings your sales team will need to undertake, it is always worth to ask a few questions:

- Will this be a completely new training for the team or is it a reinforcement and refresher (meaning reminder)?
- Will it apply to everyone in the team or just a few specific individuals?
- What specific problems we want that training to address? And why do we need that training to begin with?
- What investment should we put into the training in terms of time and money?

It doesn't hurt either to hear the opinion of the salespeople themselves by asking the simple question "What would you like to do better?"

Once those questions are answered, the company can decide how to go about the methodology of the training, and choose to go either with in-house training or outsourced training.

1. Do-it-yourself training.

Training can be developed by the HR manager in coordination with the sales manager. It is inexpensive in terms of finances, but it is time consuming to develop. The advantage is that the training will be customized and will be delivered by an

机、驾驶叉车等。

2. 第三方培训。

请培训公司的好处是他们会给你们的团队引入一些全新的技能，这些新技能可能是你们的销售团队之前没有用过的。由于他们也向其他公司提供培训服务，所以他们通常都会分享来自其他市场或领域的最佳实例，这也是培训公司的优势之一。他们有些会提供数字化的学习方案，不过我个人并不太热衷于此，因为不与听众进行互动是无法传授谈判要领的。

建议选择委托培训公司或者擅长销售和谈判的专业培训师或引导师。

3. 客户培训。

我之前曾在一家供应链公司任职，这家公司会为其客户和潜在客户组织常规的培训。培训诸如医疗保健物流或石油天然气物流之类的内容。这些培训旨在培养客户并让他们随着市场趋势保持与时俱进。更为重要的是，客户培训可以让我们的销售代表与现有的以及潜在的客户坐在一起，与他们交谈，回答他们的担忧，了解他们的业务并与他们建立联系。

insider who knows exactly what challenges are faced by the business. A good example of "do-it-yourself" is the "anti-bureaucratic week" that IKEA organizes every year. During that week, all managers have to wear sales clerk's uniforms and do everything from operating cash registers to driving forklifts.

2. Third-party training.

The advantage of using the services of a training company is that they introduce a new set of skills that were probably un-used within your sales team. Since they deliver trainings to other companies as well, they are generally able to share best practices from different markets or different industries. And that's one advantage of using them. Some of them offer e-learning, but I'm not a big fan of that. You just can't teach negotiation without interacting with the audience.

It is recommended to commission training companies or specialized trainers/facilitators that specialize in sales and negotiation.

3. Customers trainings.

I worked in the past for a supply chain company that used to organize regular trainings for its customers and prospects. Those were called Global Logistics Counciland tackles specifics such as Healthcare logistics or Oil and Gas logistics. Those trainings aim at educating customers and updating them on the latest market trends. More importantly, it allowed our sales representatives to sit at the same table with existing and potential customers, talk to them, answer their concerns, understand their businesses, and build relationships.

成为一个称职的销售经理

在上一部分你可能已经了解了销售经理职位的重要性以及他们在雇用、评估、留住员工和辅导销售代表方面的重要意义。一个销售团队没有一位称职的销售经理是无法成功的。在许多公司里，公司的老板同时也是销售经理。这对小公司也同样适用，但随着公司的成长，该职位就需要变成一份“全职工作”，公司便需要有一个人来填补这个职位。

无论你是正在寻求改善的销售经理，还是一名努力工作想要成为销售经理的有志销售代表，你都可以在后面的内容里找到一些值得借鉴的指导。

我们先来谈谈从销售代表变成销售经理，你的生活将会发生什么样的变化。作为一名销售代表，你的目标是塑造你自己。而作为一名销售经理，你的目标将变成培养其他人。你将会慢慢卸去日常事务，并开始根据你的知识和近年来积累的经验为你的团队提供指导。你将负责构建一个大家能够有所作为的工作平台。销售经理在不同的组织里有着不同的任务，但是有些任务是相同的，无论你处在哪个行业里。作为一名销售经理，你的主要任务是：

- 持续地进行公司内部和外部招聘和面试，以寻找有潜力的新员工；
- 确保有充足的销售人员，从而有效地对接客户并实现销售目标；
- 为每个销售代表创建并管理个人技能发展计划；
- 开发、制定并复查销售策略同时确保所需资源各就其位，以为销售代表的成功提供支持；
- 陪同销售代表参加可能出现复杂局面的重要谈判；
- 创建并管理销售部门预算；

Duties of a sales manager

You probably understand from the last pages the importance of the sales manager's position, and the instrumental role he plays in hiring, assessing, retaining, and coaching sales representatives. No sales team can succeed without a capable sales manager. In many companies, the business owner is also the sales manager. That could work for small structures, but as the business grows, that position will need to become a "full time job" and one person should be assigned to fill it.

Whether you are a sales manager currently looking into improving the way you work, or an ambitious sales representative working hard to get promoted to that position, you will find in the coming pages a few points to give you guidance.

First let's talk about what will exactly change in your life as you move from the sales representative position to the sales manager one. As a sales representative, your goal was to build yourself. As a sales manager, your goal will be to build other people. You will be removed slowly from the day-to-day tasks and start giving directions to your team based on the knowledge and experience you have accumulated on the ground for the last several years. You will be in charge of creating an environment in which people can and do make a difference. The tasks of a sales manager vary from one organization to another, but some of the tasks remain the same no matter what industry you operate in. Your main tasks as a Sales Manager would be to:

- Continually recruit and interview internally and externally to find new potential candidates.
- Secure sufficient sales personnel to effectively engage the customers and reach targets.
- Create and manage individual skill development plans for each sales representative.
- Develop, orchestrate, and review the sales strategy and ensure required

- 每周安排内部销售会议以检查销售状况与关键绩效指标（KPI）；
- 在整个销售周期中处理出现的各种复杂问题；
- 确保所有的新客户都以新客户的身份接受了内部的评估和讨论；
- 向管理层或股东提供及时的信息更新。

从以上要点可以看出，你的大部分时间要贡献给辨识或者优化部门内的“明星”。这也是销售经理作为一个领导岗位的原因所在。

resources are in place for the sales representatives to succeed.

- Accompany individual sales representatives to important sales meetings where complex negotiations might take place.
- Create and manage the Sales Department budget.
- Conduct weekly internal Sales Meetings to review sales measurements and performance indicators (KPI).
- Act on complex issues that emerge throughout the sales cycle.
- Ensure all new customers are reviewed and discussed internally as they are welcomed as new customers.
- Provide timely updates to management or shareholders as requested.

As you can see from the above points, most of your time will be dedicated to identifying, or otherwise building and perfecting "stars" within the department. And that's why the position of a sales manager is truly a leadership position.

合理使用客户维护经费

我想通过回答一个最近在中国经常听到的问题来结束这一部分。那个问题是关于销售人员应该如何花费他们的“客户招待”经费的。

礼品是一种建立关系和减轻商业紧张气氛的有效方式。然而，为防止滥用，许多我曾共事过的公司对礼物的类型和价值都有着严格的规定。我之前的一位客户就曾要求我们开展“反腐败”和“反贿赂”培训，包括津贴和商业礼品。于是我们不得不将该培训引入公司内部并让所有的员工都获得认证。我们要求每个员工：任何礼品往来，哪怕是额定值内的招待事宜都要经过直属经理的许可。虽然这个流程费时费力，不过在最后，我们很高兴客户们认真地把他们的业务派给了最合适的竞标者，而不是最腐败的那个。

每个销售部门都应该为礼品和客户招待设立一个预算。有些公司把邀请客户共进丰盛晚餐作为一种招待的方式。如果是我的话，通常会建议使用一种不一样的方式。我会找一家提供企业培训的公司并和他们一起设计包含培训、会议和趣味活动的一日活动，然后邀请我的客户参加。培训包括如何更好地服务客户，如何建立伙伴关系，如何为明年做计划等。培训机会是无限的。你可以称这一天为客户答谢日，或者联谊会，或是联合培训会，这些都不重要。真正重要的是其内容以及你想达到的目标。到访10~12位宾客，早上3个小时的培训，下午3个小时的研讨会，中间有一顿丰盛的午餐，你能做的远不止一天的惬意时光和有意义的商业交往。你甚至还可以将这些活动放到星期六进行。你最终将得到很多关于客户的有用信息。本该是高层领导之间的丰盛晚餐变为了一天的培训时光，来自两

Sales department expenses

I would like to conclude this section by answering a question that I have been getting a lot lately in China. It is related to the way salespeople should go about expensing their "customer entertainment" budget.

Gifts are a powerful way to build relationships and ease tensions in business. However, in order to avoid abuses, many companies I have worked with have strict guidelines regarding what gifts can be offered and of what value they can be. One of my former customers made it a requirement for us to develop a training specific to "anti-corruption" and "anti-bribery", including facilitation payments and business gifts. Then we had to deliver that training internally to every one of our employees and get all our employees certified. We also made it a requirement for anyone of our employees that any giving or receiving of gifts or entertainment of even nominal value were to be approved by their direct manager. This process was costly and time consuming but at the end, we were happy that the customer was serious about awarding their business to the most suitable bidder, not to the most corrupt one.

Every sales department should have a budget set aside for gifts and customer entertainment. Some companies call lavish dinners with customers an entertainment. When it's up to me, I generally suggest a different approach. I would find a company that delivers corporate trainings, and work with them to design a day of trainings and conferences and fun events to which I invite my customer. A training about how to better serve customers, how to build partnerships, how to make plans for next year... Training opportunities are limitless. You can call that day a Customer Appreciation Day or Relationship Building Event or Joint Training Session. It doesn't matter. What matters is the content and the goal you have in mind. With 10~12 guests, 3 hours of trainings in the morning and 3 hours of workshops in the afternoon with a good lunch in between, that can be more than enough to have a wonderful time and meaningful exchanges. You can even do it on a Saturday. You will end up learning a lot more about your customer.

家公司包括运营团队、销售团队、客服团队在内的所有人都聚到了一起，互相交流，从彼此的视角看待业务。而这样的花费可能与5星级酒店的一顿丰盛晚餐相差无几。

与一些客户重复进行几次这样的活动后你就会明白其中的奥妙所在。我在中国尝试过，并获得了令人称奇的效果。如果你想要我推荐一些我曾合作过、能提供这方面优质服务的公司的话，可以来联系我。

我曾听到许多人说："嗯，这些想法听起来不错，也很合理，但是它们只在西方世界有效。"我不敢苟同。它们可能在有些文化中需要些时间适应才能真正实施，但最终在哪里都是行得通的。我没见到过有哪个客户会拒绝一次"免费"优质的培训。

The lavish dinner that was supposed to be held between the top executives ends up being a one-day training where operation teams, sales teams, customer service teams from both companies are all brought together to get to know each other and understand business from each other's perspective. And that could probably cost your company as much as the lavish dinner in the 5 stars hotel.

Repeat that a few times with a few customers and see how wonderful the dynamics become. I have done it in China and it worked wonders. Don't hesitate to get in touch with me if you'd like me to recommend companies I worked with in the past and have delivered an excellent service.

I heard many people saying "well, these ideas are fine and sound, but they would only work in a Western culture." I beg to differ. They might take more time to implement in some cultures than in others, but they would ultimately work anywhere. I don't see any customer in his right mind declining a "free" good quality training for his team.

| 第三部分 |

老外眼中的中国销售

在与中国的诸多出口公司共事时，我曾遇到过一些生产优质产品的好公司。遗憾的是，在这些公司当中有许多都在营销前端或客服前端显露出了明显的弱点。这也不禁让我思考，如果没有一种有效的营销手段展示其产品真正的价值，就不会有人知道这款产品，那生产如此出色的产品又有什么意义呢？同样的，拥有一个好产品、一个出色的销售流程，却也有一个一旦交易完成就不再对客户的任何问题和要求负责的糟糕售后服务，这样又意义何在呢？

| Part 3 |

Chinese Salespeople Through a Foreigner's Eyes

In my work with countless exporting businesses here in China, I came across some wonderful companies that make outstanding quality products. Sadly, for many of them, they showed clear weakness on the marketing front or the customer service front. It made me wonder what was the point of making an amazing product if no one knows about it through an efficient marketing that demonstrates the true value of that product. And what was the point of having a good product, a good sales process, but a bad after-sales service that doesn't insure that the customer's expectations are exceeded even after the transaction is completed.

与中国销售打交道时常遇到的 14 个问题

我准备在这里列举一些在不同的语境下，我从中国的销售人员那儿听到的错误陈述，然后我会解释作为一名外国人我是如何理解这些话的。我在后面给出了一小段优化后的表述方式，为你提供类似场景下的对话参考。

场景 1　卖家："杰里向我同时也向总经理、副总以及分部经理汇报工作。"

我的想法：我是卖家，如果杰里不能解决我的问题，谁能？如果他休病假，谁来接替他？

建议：始终在电子邮件结尾附上你的名字、联系方式，还有你的直属经理的联系方式。如果某位客户对你的服务感到满意，他便能找到一个可以分享其积极反馈的人。对服务不满意的客户通常不会告诉你他们的想法，他们只会直接离开。如果某位客户对你这个层级的服务不满意，他会去找你的直属经理表达愤怒，而不是离开。

场景 2　卖家："抱歉，这是公司的政策。"

我的想法：别啰唆了，没有人在意你公司的政策，解决好我的问题就行。

建议：你们公司的政策与我无关。你的以上陈述会向客户传递出你不懂变通而且不愿帮助他的意思。有时候打破常规是很有必要的。如果你的公司不能为客户破例，你的竞争者便会这么做。一种更好的方式是这么表述的："这是我们有这个规定的原因所在（此处解释原因），我们可以为您找找解决

The 14 Challenges I encountered when dealing with Chinese salespeople

I decided to list here some of the wrong statements I heard from sales people in China in different contexts, then explain what went in my foreigner's mind when I heard them. I then suggest a short and better way to frame the discussion should similar situations happen to you.

Situation 1 Seller: "Jerry reports to me, and at the same time to the General Manager, to the VP, and to the Branch Manager."

My mind: I'm a buyer, and if Jerry can't solve my problem, who can? If he is on sick leave, who would step in to cover for him?

Suggestion: Always add at the end of your emails your name, your contact information, and the contact information of your direct manager. If a customer is happy with your level of service, he will find someone to share his positive feed-back with. Unhappy customers don't always tell you they are unhappy. They just walk away. If the customer is not satisfied with your level of service, instead of walking away, he will find your direct manager to absorb his anger.

Situation 2 Seller: "Sorry, this is the company's policy."

My mind: Newsflash, no one cares about your policy. Just fix my problem.

Suggestion: Your company's policies are your company's, not mine. Your above statement sends a signal to the customer that you are not flexible and

这个问题的其他方法"。

场景 3 卖家："你从没告诉我这是一个问题！"

我的想法：在我转向其他的竞争者前，辨识客户的痛点应该是你们的工作。

建议：除非你曾与客户保持密切联系，否则你永远都不知道客户的问题是什么，一直都是如此。根据商业规模的不同，一般会每隔 3 个月、6 个月或者 12 个月在客户服务评价或业务回顾的过程中来了解客户的问题。当你保持这些沟通渠道的开放时，客户就会在有改善需求的时候向你直言其问题所在。如果你不这么做的话，他就会在市场上寻找其他的服务提供者（比如你的直接竞争对手）。一旦他找到了你的竞争对手，他就会向其诉说你们公司的服务有多糟糕。

我比较愿意听到销售人员这么说："我们愿意和您每隔 3 个月进行一次会面并对我们的业务合作进行评估。"

场景 4 卖家："我们核验过了，我们已经发货。谢谢！再见！"

我的想法：我就知道那个销售代表只是想要我的钱而已！

建议：货物运输并到达目的地后，你不妨给我打个电话并问问货物是否完好，以及我是否满意。这会让我感受到你们的真诚。理想情况下，这个电话还能帮你获取更多的信息，比如询问货物的最终目的地是哪里，或者他们如何使用这批货物。我一般喜欢更进一步地询问客户："如果您觉得我们在处理这次交易时还有某个地方有待提高，您觉得会是什么呢？"

unwilling to help him. Sometimes making exceptions is a necessity. If your company doesn't make those exceptions, your competitor would. A better way to frame it would be to say: "Here is the reason why we have that rule in place (explain the reason here). Let us explore other ways to solve this for you".

Situation 3 Seller: "You never told me this was a problem!"

My mind: It's your job to identify my pain points before I start talking about them to the competition.

Suggestion: You will never know the customer's problems unless you keep your fingers on his pulse all the time. That happens through customer service reviews or business reviews that take place every 3 months or 6 months or 12 months, depending on the size of the business. When you keep those lines of communication open, the customer will confess to you where he needs you to improve. When you don't, be sure that he is out there in the market looking for another supplier (likely your direct competitor). Once he finds your competitor, he will tell them how bad your service is.

What I would like to hear salespeople say is "We would like to meet with you once every 3 months to assess where our relationship stands".

Situation 4 Seller: "We got the check. We shipped. Thank you. Bye."

My mind: That sales representative only wants my money. I knew it!

Suggestion: Once the goods are shipped and arrive at the destination, it doesn't hurt if you pick-up the phone and ask me if the goods were well received and if I'm happy with them. This tells me that you genuinely care. Ideally, that call you have placed will help you gather more information by inquiring further about the final destination of the goods, or the usage that would be made of them. I generally like to push this one step further and tell the customer "if there was one thing we could

场景 5 卖家:“抱歉，这是销售部门，不是客服部门。”

我的想法：客户服务不是一个部门，而是一种态度。

建议：无论客户给公司的哪个人打了电话，他都应该得到那个人的认真聆听。公司里的每一个人都是公司的形象代表。如果你可以为客户提供快速的现场回答，那没问题。如果你不能，那就问问该客户具体遇到了哪方面的问题，并提议将电话转接到合适的员工那里。我一般会说：“我明白了您的问题。请让我为您转接到设计部门的大卫先生那儿，他将可以帮到您。为防止电话断线，请留下您的电话号码，这样我们就能够联系到您。”

场景 6 卖家:“我们的职员每 3 个月轮换一次，不过不用担心，我们的业务状况良好。”

我的想法：每次你们公司和我联系的直接联系人都在变，我觉得无所适从。

建议：客户并不是从公司而是从公司的职员那儿购买产品或服务。没有什么比向供应商解释完需求，然后一周后被告知之前的联系对象变了更让人心烦的了，因为我不得不重新解释一遍。没有人愿意花这个时间。那些有长期固定员工的公司会让我觉得其是一家稳定的公司，并旨在与客户建立良好的长期合作关系。

场景 7 卖家:“我们做不了，但我还是要接下这笔生意。”

我的想法：别告诉我你们公司专门制造智能手机、椅子、卡车、玩具和

improve in the way I handled this transaction, what would that be?"

Situation 5 Seller: "Sorry, this is the sales department, not the customer service department."

My mind: Customer service is an attitude, not a department.

Suggestion: If a customer calls anyone within the company, he should find a listening person at the other end of the line. Every single employee within the company is the voice and the face of the company. If you could provide a quick on the spot answer, do it. If not, ask the customer what kind of challenge he is exactly facing, and propose to direct them to the right person. What I would say is "I got your point. Let me try to direct you to Mr David from design department who would be able to help you. Just in case the call drops, let me note down your phone number so we can call you back."

Situation 6 Seller: "Our employees rotate every 3 months, but don't worry, we are good."

My mind: Every time my direct contact within your company changes, I panic.

Suggestion: Customers don't buy from companies, they buy from people. Nothing frustrates me more than explaining my requirements to the supplier, to hear the following week that my direct contact I was communicating with has been replaced by another employee, and that I have to go through the same explanation process again. No one has time for that. Companies with long-time serving employees tell me that your company is a stable company geared towards building long-term relationships.

Situation 7 Seller: "I can't do that, but I'll take the business anyway."

My mind: Don't tell me that your factory specializes in manufacturing

化学制品，还都是同时进行的！

建议：在中国，“中间人”颇为兴盛。我曾遇到过问我是否有兴趣买水管的出租车司机。真的！如果你无法做某件事，不妨清楚地告诉对方。我对那些告诉我“这不是我们能够提供的服务，但是我们可以为您推荐几家可能对你有帮助的公司”的销售人员是怀有很高敬意的。

场景 8　卖家：“我们已经和您连续合作 2 年了，让我们一直按这样的方式合作下去吧。”

我的想法：在这期间我已经和其他的供应商谈好了。他们会带来不错的收益，我想试试和他们合作。

建议：想当然地对待任何一场交易是不安全的，无论你和当前的客户有着多么深厚的合作关系。如果是明智的客户，他会在市场上寻找更好的合作对象，而且有大量的公司能为其提供服务。因此一直寻找留住和愉悦现有客户的新方式是很有必要的。时刻做好准备回答客户这样的提问：“你们除此之外还能为我做什么”或者“你们还能为我提供什么价值”。我以前用的方法是：“成本节约计划”。我大约每隔 6 个月与客户见一次面，为他们提供改善目前合作状况的方案，这样可以节省他们的开支。我会说：“我相信贵公司和我们的合作非常愉快。我们愿意通过这个成本节约计划来推进进一步的合作。”

场景 9　卖家：“我们的价格比竞争对手高 3 倍，但是我们的品质要比他们好 10 倍。”

我的想法：严明的公司会给他们的销售团队设一个底价并设一个不会让

smartphones, chairs, trucks, toys, and chemicals, all at the same time!

Suggestion: The business of "middle-man" is a very prosperous one in China. I have met taxi drivers who asked me if I was interested in buying water-pumps. Seriously! If you can't do something, it doesn't hurt to state it clearly. I have high respect for a salesperson that would tell me "This is not a service we could offer, but we can suggest one or two companies that might be able to assist you".

Situation 8 Seller: "We have been doing consistent business with you for 2 years now. Let's keep doing what we've always done."

My mind: Meanwhile, I have been talking to this and that other supplier. They offer good value and I would like to try them.

Suggestion: It is unsafe to take any business for granted. It doesn't matter how strong your relationship with your existing customer is. If he is wise, he is out there in the market looking for better deals and it is very likely that there are plenty of companies to service him. Hence it is of high importance to always find new ways to retain and entertain existing customers. Always have an answer for the customer that asks "What else can you do for me?" or "What other value could you offer me?" The approach I have used in the past is "cost saving plans". I would go back to my customer every 6 months or so and propose how we can improve the way we do business so the value of the invoices they pay is lower. I would say: "We believe your company has had a positive experience working with us. We would like to take that to the next level by implementing this cost-saving plan."

Situation 9 Seller: "Our price is three times higher than the competition but we're ten times better."

My mind: Serious companies fix a minimum price for their sales team and a

客户产生被欺骗感的最高价格。

建议：每个销售人员都明白自己所售产品的价格底线。那么价格上限在哪呢？假设某件商品的价值是 10 美元，在同样的商品和条件下你向我要价 20 美元，那我会说你是骗子并径直走开。即使你以 20 美元的价格卖给了我，我最后也会发现其实这件商品的价值应该是 10 美元，于是我就会回来与你理论。同时我还会到处宣扬自己在你们公司被骗的经历。事实是，在各种线上平台日益发达的今天，想要抬高商品的标准价格变得越来越难。有这样一个例子，我曾工作过的一家公司设置了有上限的标准定价，如果谁向客户的要价超过上限就会被视为不道德。当有销售代表以高于这个内部设定的价格卖出了一件产品，他的经理就会找到相应客户致以歉意并补偿差价。

场景 10　卖家："我们遇到一个大问题所以无法按原计划交货了。抱歉。"

我的想法：谢谢你的坏消息，但是解决方案呢？或者你是打算让我替你找到办法吗？

建议：客户在听到坏消息时是很不安的。不过他们会在听到你提出的建议和解决方案后恢复平静。任何人都可能打电话告诉我他们在生产过程中所面临的挑战，但不是所有人都能够告诉我他们将如何解决问题以及保全我的商业利益。你的客户将你视为他们的一名销售顾问，而不仅仅是一个销售代表。提供解决方案和设想也是你工作职责的一部分，在这个过程中你不仅可以获得这笔交易还能获得经济回报。

我一般会这么说："我们在 ×× 部分遇到了一些挑战。作为临时解决方案，我们会启用合约里提过的应急计划。我们会在 24 小时内再次联系您并给

maximum price above which the customer would feel cheated.

Suggestion: Every salesman knows the lowest price under which he can not sell his product. But how about the highest price? If the value of a commodity is 10, and you propose to offer me the same commodity under the same terms but for 20, then I will walk away and call you cheater. Even if you manage to sell me that commodity for 20, and I realize later on that it actually was supposed to be 10, I will go back to you to argue over this. I will also broadcast it everywhere that I have been cheated by your company. The truth is, with all the online platforms available today, it's getting harder and harder to overprice standard goods, but the practice is still there. A company I worked for in the past had capped standard pricing and it was deemed unethical to charge a customer above that cap. If a sales representative sold a product at a price higher than the internally set price, his manager would go back to the customer to apologize and reimburse the difference.

Situation 10 Seller: "We have a big problem to deliver as we agreed. Sorry about that."

My mind: Thanks for the bad news, but what's the solution? Or are you expecting me to find solutions on your behalf?

Suggestion: Customers will freak out when they hear a bad news. But they will calm down once they hear the resolution you suggest. Anybody can call me about a challenge they are facing during the production, but not everybody can tell me how they intend to solve it and how my business interests will be preserved. Your customers expect you to act as a sales consultant rather than just a sales representative. Providing solutions and ideas is part of your duties. In exchange, you will get my business and my money.

The way I would frame it would be something that goes like this: "We are facing some challenges with × × area. As a temporary solution, we will activate the contingency plan referenced in our agreement. We will get back to you within the

出一份包含问题分析、解决方案以及防止此类问题再次发生的举措在内的完整文件。"

场景 11　卖家："噢，你们想知道这个工厂是否完工了？差不多吧。"

我的想法：这些人在隐藏什么。

建议：在外国人的思维里，要么就是完成了，要么就是没完成但是会在 ×× 时间内完成。不确定性是很可怕的，因为我认识的每个有经验的销售人员都有 1 年、3 年、5 年计划等。如果某件事与"差不多"产生关联，那么这个商人就会失信并面临商业危机。他经常做的事就是转移到他更安全的 B 计划上，而你就只能被拖累着，自己干着急。

我过去曾这样说过："我们已经 100% 完成了阶段 1、阶段 2 和阶段 3。阶段 4 已经完成了 80%，目前正在等待政府的进程许可。我们预计会在接下来的 2 到 3 周内完成。"

场景 12　卖家："我们正面临着一个大问题。"

我的想法：哦不！你们又要让我失望了。

建议："问题"是商人生活的一部分。不过不同的人在听到"问题"一词后会有不一样的反应。一般来说，一个理智的人在听到你提及"问题"的时候是不会微笑或者表现出愉悦的。这也是为什么我建议在你所有的交流中都不要用"问题"这个词，用"挑战"会更好。当我们说"挑战"的时候，我们也在暗示这是可以克服的，传递出一种只要我们努力就能改善的信息。我们已经通过使用积极的语言迈出了向积极模式转变的第一步。

coming 24 hours with a full analysis of what happened, how we will respond, and what we will do to prevent this from happening again."

Situation 11 Seller: "Oh you're inquiring about the completion of the plant? It's complete, Cha Bu Duo."

My mind: These guys are hiding something.

Suggestion: In the foreigner's mind, either something is done or not yet done but will be done within × × time. Uncertainty is scary because every seasoned businessman I have known has a 1-year plan, a 3-year plan, a 5-year plan...When something is filed under the "chabuduo" category, the businessman loses visibility and his business is at risk. What he often does is move to his safer Plan B and let you hang there high and dry.

What I have said in the past is: "We have completed phase 1, phase 2 and phase 3 at 100%. Phase 4 is completed at 80%, and we are pending Government's approval to proceed. We expect to get it within the coming 2 to 3 weeks".

Situation 12 Seller: "We are facing a major problem."

My mind: Oh no, you will let me down again.

Suggestion: "Problems" are part of the businessman's life. But different people have different reactions when they hear the word "problem". In general, a reasonable person will not smile and act happy when you mention the word"problem." That's why I suggest getting rid of the word "problem" altogether in all your communications, and favoring the usage of the word "challenge". When we say "challenge", we are hinting to something that could be overcome, a situation that could only get better and improve if we act on it. We are already using a positive language as a first step towards setting a positive mood.

场景 13 卖家："我们是中国最好的玩具制造商。"

我的想法：我今天在展会上已经听到这样的话 4 次了。

建议：与上述类似的言论是不会让你的公司看起来比其他公司更可信的，事实恰好相反。我们都知道只有少数的几家大型公司在它们所在的领域可以称得上是"中国最好"。但是如果不指明是在哪个确切领域做得最好的话，那也说明不了什么问题。你的客户服务最好，产品质量最好，还是最创新？只有在有事实支持的情况下这些陈述才有意义，比如说政府的嘉奖或者知名机构的证书等。

场景 14 卖家："抱歉，我们最近因为一个优质客户的大订单而异常忙碌。"

我的想法：如果我和他们做生意，那他们会将我视为一名次要客户。

建议：当一名销售人员说了以上的话时，他的本意通常不坏。他只是想告诉你他们的公司很成功而且他们的产品很畅销。只是他用了一种错误的方式。我听到的是"我们无法承受大订单，因为仅仅一个就够我们折腾的了"或者"你的订单太小了，所以我们不是很在意。请让我们继续处理我们的大客户吧"。你不必告诉你的客户你很忙碌，他可能早就心里有数了。

Situation 13 Seller: "We are the best toy makers in China."

My mind: I have heard this statement 4 times today in this exhibition.

Suggestion: Claims similar to the above one do not make your company look more credible than others. They make it look less credible. We all know that there are only a handful large companies that can claim "they are the best in China" in whatever they are doing. Being the best doesn't say much if it doesn't state clearly in which field you are best. Are you the best in customer service? The best in quality? The best in innovation? Similar statements would make sense only if they are backed by actual facts such as a Government award, or a reputable institution's certificate that proves the claim.

Situation 14 Seller: "Sorry we have been busy lately with a large order we got from a good customer."

My mind: If I give them my business, they will treat me as a second-class customer.

Suggestion: When a salesperson says the above sentence, his intention is often good. He is trying to convey the fact that their company is a successful one and its products are on high demand. He unfortunately is conveying it the wrong way. What I hear is "We can not handle big orders because we just had one and we are struggling" or "Your business is too small so we will not care much about you. Let us deal with our large clients". You don't need to tell your customer you're busy. He probably already knows.

如何好好处理与外国客户的关系

对中国企业来说，要想与国外企业建立成功的商业关系，知道**如何与外国客户以及外国潜在客户沟通**至关重要，这也正是本书第一部分的主题。同时，在与外国客户进行远程交涉，或当有外国客户来华拜访你时，明白要**如何表现**也很重要。对方在见到你的第一时间就会形成对你的印象。因此在最开始的时候通过正确的做事方式给对方留下一个好印象非常重要，这也是第三部分的主题所在。

请记住，学习如何对待外国与你职位相当的客户并不是你单方面的付出。明智的外国人也会在来中国之前搜集一些有关这个国家及现有环境的信息，并试着理解当地商业的基本运作方式。他们甚至还会参加研讨班学习如何在中国或者与中国商人做生意。如果他们没有这么做，我们可以帮助他们。为你的外国客人提供一本有关“中国文化”或“中国商业”的书便是一个能够帮助他们了解中国的不错方式。

话虽这么说，但当你在世界各地旅行时你会发现在所有的文化里，基本的礼仪几乎都是相同的。比如保持清洁、不说谎、说话平缓、学会倾听、感恩、为别人留门、坐姿端正、合适的眼神交流以及积极向上的态度等。

现在就来看看一些中国商人对待外国访客时应注意的地方吧。

提示 1: 可以说“不”

我所经历的中国文化是没有对抗性的。在与中国人交流时，他们一般都

Do you know how to deal well with your foreign clients

It is important for Chinese businesses to know **how to communicate** with foreign clients and foreign potential clients in order to make for a successful business relationship. This was the topic of the first part. It is equally important to know **how to act** when dealing with foreign clients remotely or foreign clients visiting you in China. People form their opinion of you from the very first moment they engage in an exchange with you. It is of the utmost importance to leave a very good impression from the very beginning by doing things the right way. This is the topic of this part.

Keep in mind that learning how to deal with a foreign counterpart is not a one-way effort. Wise foreigners coming to China also gather knowledge about the country and the environment prior to their arrival and try to gain a basic understanding of how things run in this side of the world. They even attend seminars on how to do business in and with China. If they don't, we can help them. Offering your foreign guest a book about "Chinese culture" or "Business in China" is a nice gesture that could help in that education process.

That being said, when traveling around the globe, you will realize that the basics of civility are almost the same in every culture. It is always good practice to encourage cleanliness, not lie, speak slowly and learn how to listen, be grateful, hold the door for others, sit straight and maintain reasonable eye contact, be positive, and so forth and so on.

Let's take a quick look at some of the areas we can start being mindful of when welcoming our foreign guests in China.

很得体且考虑周全。他们很少会直视我的眼睛，也很少说出他们对我或者我提的条件不满意的地方。他们会以其他的形式表达分歧，并由我来决定是否要试着去解读或解释他们所传达出的信号。我告诉我的中国朋友，我是一个商人，尽管很棘手，我也需要一个诚实的反馈。当然也包括大多数的外国人。如果你们的公司与来自北欧国家的公司有过往来，那你们应该已经接触过这些地方直接坦率的文化了。即使对一个外国买家明确地说“抱歉我们做不到”，也没有谁会受到什么伤害。但当你说“这可能有点困难”时，你会给你的外国听众传递错误的信息。对我而言这可能意味着“虽然有点难，但我们还是会努力去做，或许可以成功”。这与“我明白这是你们的需求，但是由于新的城市规定，我们没有做这个的权限”还是有很大差别的。如果这看起来太直白，可以在这句话的前面加一点积极的论调，传递的也是相同的信息，比如说：“我明白这是你们的需求。我们很希望能为您提供这样的服务，您也知道，我们一直以来都按照你们的要求来做，不过因为新的城市规定，我们不再有这么做的权限了。”

在许多文化里，保持沉默并非是表达分歧的一种标准方式，不过在中国是这样的。我曾遇到过对方没有回答我的观点或问题的情况，我很疑惑为什么对方要忽视我。后来我才明白当时对方给了我回答，而回答是否定的。在这些情况中，没有回答意味着“不”。这虽然不至于让我的中国客户显得无礼，但会让像我一样的外国人感到不自在。

提示 2: 不妨直接问问客户的饮食习惯

印度人吃什么样的食物？穆斯林不吃什么肉？瑞典人喜欢火锅吗？答案很简单：直接问他们！你不妨在他们到达之前就问问他们，然后为其准备相

Pointer 1: It's OK to say "no"

Chinese culture as I have come to experience it is not confrontational. People in China are very diplomatic and considerate in their interactions. They would rarely look at me straight in the eyes and tell me everything they don't like about me or what I'm offering. They would rather express their disagreement in other forms, and it's up to me to try to read and interpret the signals. I tell my Chinese friends that I'm a businessman and can handle a tough but honest feed-back. And so do most foreigners. If your company has dealt with partners originating from Northern European countries, it is likely that you have experienced the straight-forward nature of those cultures. No one would get hurt when a foreign buyer is told a clear "Sorry we can not do that". When you say instead "This might be a little difficult to do", you send the wrong message to the foreign listeners. For me it might mean "It is difficult to do it but we will try to make it anyways and we will maybe succeed". Very different from the "I understand this is what you need, but given the new city regulations, we are not authorized to do it." If this seems too confrontational, the same meaning could be conveyed by adding a positive tone at the beginning of the sentence. Something like "I understand this is what you need. We would have loved to provide that service to you. You know, we've always done it the way you requested it, but given the new city regulations, we are not authorized to do it anymore."

In many cultures, staying silent is not a standard answer to express disagreement, but in China it is. I have run into situations where my messages or questions were not being answered, leaving me wondering why I was being ignored. I found out later that this meant the answer to my requests was negative, and no answer in those cases just meant "no". This doesn't make my Chinese counterparts disrespectful, but it just creates some uneasiness for the foreigner that I am.

应的食物以迎合他们的饮食习惯。你会发现有些外国访客是天性好奇的，因此并不排斥新奇的异域食品。有些则不是，在涉及吃的时候，他们还是比较喜欢待在自己的舒适区里。所以为确保万无一失，还是先问问他们比较好。我曾在美国参加过一次会议，当时该会议的组织者让我提前几天告诉他们我对午餐和晚餐是否有什么特殊的需求。一般来说，我知道鸡腿、蛇汤以及鱼头都不是外国人的日常食物，所以要避开这些。我很喜欢吃火锅，而且我并不在意大家围坐在一起把各自的筷子浸在同一个锅里。但是有些外国人很在意，所以最好也不要选择这个。我记得第一次在中国吃火锅是由一对中国夫妇款待的。在开始之前，他们给我大致讲了下餐桌的座序、筷子的使用、食物的解释、中国人的习惯等。如果大家都这样的话，交流就会容易许多吧。在对待外国访客时也是一样的道理。我们最不希望发生的事是与一名饿着肚子的买家谈判，或者更糟的是，与一名吃了四川火锅后胃不太舒服的买家谈判。

在中国，饭桌的座序是很重要的。中国的主人会在大家进入房间后为每人分配座位。外国人并不了解这些，他们可能会走进来后直接选个地方坐下来。如果发生这样的情况，他们真的不是有意冒犯！

提示 3：结束时间同样重要

据我回忆，我从未收到过一封来自中国销售员注明了开始和结束时间的请帖或会议请求，好像所有的会议都只有一个开始时间，都没有加上结束时间的习惯。在美国从商的这些年，我听到的都是“我们的会议从 15：30 到 16：30”，而不是“我们约定在 15：30 见面”。在接待一名外国客户前，强烈建议你在他们到达前给他们一个大致的日程。可以是一封列有你想做的事

Pointer 2: There is no harm in asking the guest about their eating habits

What kind of food can an Indian eat? What meat a Muslim person is not allowed to eat? Do Swedish people like hot pot? The answer is simple: Just ask them! It doesn't hurt to ask the foreign visitor prior to their arrival what arrangements can be made to meet their eating habits. You'll find out that some foreign visitors are curious by nature, and don't fear trying new and exotic foods. Some others are not. They prefer to stay in their comfort zone when it comes to eating. So it is always safe to ask. I have participated in conferences in the US where I was asked by the organizers a few days in advance to notify them of any special arrangements I needed for lunch and dinner. In general, I know that chicken legs, snake soup, and fish head are not common food among foreigners, so it's safe to avoid them. I love hot pot and I don't mind having everyone around the table dipping their chopsticks into the same pot. Some foreigners do mind that and it is preferred to avoid it. I remember the first hot pot dinner I had in China. It was graciously offered by a Chinese couple. Before proceeding, they gave me a small overview of the sitting arrangements around the table, the chopstick usage, the food served, the Chinese habits, and so forth. This made life easier for all of us. The same could be done with any foreign visitor to make the eating experience a pleasant one. The last thing we want is to negotiate with a buyer with an empty stomach, or worse, a buyer with an upset stomach after eating a Sichuan spicy soup.

The sitting arrangements are important around the Chinese table. The Chinese host will be in charge of assigning seats once everyone enters the room. Foreigners are not aware of those arrangements. They might walk in and sit down right away at a seat of their choice. Don't feel offended when this occurs!

Pointer 3: The finishing time is as important as the starting time

As far as I could recall, I have never received an invitation or meeting request

情或者希望与他们共同达成的事项的电子邮件。一旦获得了他们的确认，就可以给他们发送日程了。一份以小时为间隔，列有目标见面人以及待办事项的日程安排就是个不错的选择。一家更为专业的公司，会在特定会议或活动后面加上希望达成的目标。以下是一个半天的例子。

周一：

08：00-08：30 与X先生、生产经理一起参观工厂，了解我们的生产流程。

08：30-09：30 会见Y先生（我们的CEO），谈谈明年的目标和举措。

09：30-11：00 与A先生和B先生参观产业园，检查之前谈过的新仓库布局。

11：00-12：00 与A、B和Z先生在WTR餐厅共进午餐。

该中国公司的商业模式和时间安排看起来都很专业，使外国买家的时间也得到了最大的优化和利用。双赢！

你如果觉得很难制订出这样的小时制日程安排，至少也要制订一个以天为单位的日程，并列出每天的主要活动以及预期结果。

出于礼貌，请记住要提前询问你的访客是否觉得该日程可行，并看他们是否希望加上或者去掉某些项目。在访问过程中，你也可以根据具体情况灵活调整这些活动。

提示4：行政事务安排

如果你在工作中遇到一个问题，你首先会找你的直属经理还是你经理的经理谈话呢？从逻辑上说，应该是你的直属经理。这是因为指挥链的存在是有理由的，遵守其运作机制也很重要。同样重要的是当你应对客户的组织机

from a Chinese salesperson that states a starting time and an ending time. It seems as if all meetings have a starting time, but none adds into it the discipline of setting an ending time. From the years I spent in business in the US, it was standard practice to hear "Let's meet from 15:30 to 16:30" rather than " Let's meet at 15:30".Before welcoming a foreign customer, it is highly recommended to suggest a rough agenda to them prior to their arrival. It could be an email that lists what you would like to do or achieve together during their visit. Once they agree to that, the next step is to send them an agenda. An hour-by-hour schedule that lists who you would meet or what you would do. A more professional company could go a step further by adding what you would like to achieve with that meeting or activity. An example of a half day is listed below.

Monday:

08:00 to 08:30 Factory visit with Mr. X, production manager, to understand our production process.

08:30 to 09:30 Meeting with our CEO Mr. Y to discuss next year targets and initiatives.

09:30 to 11:00 Visit of the Industrial Park with Mr. A and Mr. B to go over the new warehouse layout previously discussed.

11:00 to 12:00 Lunch at Restaurant WTR with Mr. A, Mr. B, and Mr. Z.

The Chinese company sounds professional in its approach to business and time. The foreign buyer's time is optimized to the maximum. Everybody wins!

If this hour-by-hour scheduling is hard to draft, it is possible to send at least a day-by-day agenda that lists the main activities of the day and the outcome expected.

Out of courtesy, remember to ask the visitor in advance if the agenda is fine with them and see if they suggest to add or remove anything from it. During the visit, it is OK to be flexible and adjust the activities as the day develops.

Pointer 4: Executive alignment

If you face a challenge at work, the first person you will go talk to would

构时，对这些运作机制的观察。各组织之间的协调有时很简单，只要让你这边合适的人去和外国客户那边合适的人对接即可。让你公司的运营主管与客户那边的前端客服代理沟通是没有太大意义的。如果有需要的话，应该让两个组织机构的前端代理与前端代理对话，管理者与管理者对话，经理与经理对话，副总与副总对话，CEO 与 CEO 对话。这一点很重要，因为高层的对话应该发生在两方的管理者之间，否则一个公司的 CEO 就得亲自拨打电话，向每一位前端代理解释他的战略目标了。虽然有时有稍微模糊这些沟通界限的必要，不过无论甲方还是乙方，都是明确的沟通和清晰的上报途径的受益者，因为这样可以让双方的交流更加顺畅。协调完成得越早，就越容易维持良好的合作关系。在许多公司里，你会发现一旦获得了一个客户，就会开始一个“过渡与实施”阶段。在这个阶段里，双方会参与讨论，一起策划流程，分配组织内部人选，制定关键绩效指标，确立付款要求等。行政事务安排的机制也正是在这个阶段逐步建立起来的。

提示 5: 做一名擅长说话的销售

我相信这个部分是中国的销售人员与外国客户交流过程中的一大障碍。我遇到过一些人不知道如何在谈判前闲聊，或者不知道如何应对交易过程中的尴尬停顿。闲聊是一种艺术，所有与手头上的交易没有直接联系的开场对话都可以视为一次闲聊。成功的闲聊可以是对你和对方分享的某件事情发表一个简单的评论。这有助于建立联系，或者是经常提及的“抛砖引玉”。如果该评论还能提供一些关于你自己的信息，那就更好了。这可以让别人也以同样的方式参与进来，并让他们分享有关自己的信息。随着讨论的进行，在之前的话题上建立新话题也就变得更加简单，与此同时也要牢记对话的过程始

be your direct manager or your manager's manager? Logically, it would be your direct manager. That's because the chain of command exists for a reason, and it's important to observe its mechanisms. It is equally important to observe those mechanisms when it comes to dealing with the customer's organization. Alignment between organizations could be as simple as getting the right people from your organization talking to the right people from the foreign customer's side. It does not make much sense having the Head of Operations from your company talking to the desk-level customer service agent from the customer's side. Desk level agents from both organizations should be talking to each other if needed, supervisors talk to supervisors, managers to managers, VP's to VP's, and CEO's to CEO's. It is important because high level discussions should take place between high level executives, otherwise it gets frustrating for a CEO to pick up the phone and explain his strategic goals to every desk-level agent. It is sometimes necessary to slightly blur those lines. But both organizations benefit from a clearly defined communication and escalation path that will smoothen the interactions between the two parties. The earliest this is done, the better the relationship will be controlled. In many companies, you will find that once a customer is acquired, a "Transition and Implementation" phase starts. During that phase, the two parties engage in discussions to map out their processes, assign roles within the organizations, define their KPIs, formalize the payment requirements…It's during this phase where the executive alignment is defined and agreed upon.

Pointer 5: Learn the basics of chit-chatting

I believe this ranks high among the areas Chinese salespeople struggle with when interacting with foreign customers. I have met several people who struggle to engage in small talk before negotiations begin, or struggle to fill in awkward pauses during the exchange. Small talk is an art. Any opening talk not directly related to the business on hand could be considered a small talk. Good small talks can start with a

终要保持一个平衡，没有哪一方会愿意花 5 分钟的时间来讲话，却仅仅得到对方 5 秒钟的回应。在交易过程中，可以用点头的方式来表现你在聆听，并以此示意对方继续讲下去。

有些人是天生的健谈者，有些则不是。但是优秀的销售人员绝对应该做到擅长交谈。我个人喜欢通过每个月参加几次社交活动特别是商业联谊会来获得练习的机会。这些活动都是销售人员练习技能的不二选择，他们可以在此试验“破冰术”、电梯法则、价值论证等的效果。在这些活动中或许还能结识新客户。

提示 6: 收集有价值的信息

我曾有一次在被一位销售经理迎接时，被问及“你们的公司是做什么的”。我刚开始还以为他在开玩笑，后来发现其实他没有。他有我的全名、电子邮件地址以及我的公司名称，但却不愿花上一点时间在网上做些调查，来看看我是否值得他投入时间，这着实让人感到尴尬。事先问问你自己一些基本的问题总是有必要的，比如：和我交易的这个人是正确的人吗？他是美国人还是仅仅居住在美国？他的背景是什么？他的专长领域是什么？如今的社交网络提供了大量的信息让你可以更好地了解那个你正面对的人。真的是这样。而且许多都是免费的，只需要你点击几下鼠标就可以。尽管如此，许多中国的职员并没有在网上查看有关客户及其业务的更多信息。总的来说，了解得更多总比什么都不知道要好。几年前，我花了好几天的时间试着联系某位客户，但是一直没能成功。我以为是她故意忽略我的电话和电子邮件。于是我去领英网搜索她的名字并试着查找一些关于她的其他信息，依旧没什么新发现。接着我又在脸谱网上输入了她的名字，结果我看到的第一幅图片就是她

simple comment about something you and the other party share. This helps creating a connection, or an “anchor” as it is often referred to. If that comment could provide some information about yourself, it’s a plus. It makes it easy for the other person to do the same and share information about themselves. As the discussion progresses, it becomes easier to build on previous comments, while keeping in mind that it is preferable to have a balance in the conversation. No one party has to spend five minutes talking while the other replies back with 5 second statements. During the exchange, head-nods could be used to show understanding and invite the other party to keep going.

Some people are born good talkers, some others are not. But good salespeople should definitely be good at it. I myself like to develop it through practicing by attending a few social events every month, especially networking events. Those events are a good practicing ground for salespeople in that they allow to test the effectiveness of our “ice-breakers”, elevator pitch, or value demonstration. These might end up being a good occasion to meet a new potential customer too.

Pointer 6: Learn how to collect valuable information

I was once welcomed by a sales manager who asked me “What does your company do?” I thought he was kidding, but he was not. He had my full name, email address, and company’s name but did not bother looking it up online to know if I’m even worth his time or not. It felt awkward. It is always worth asking yourself some basic questions such as: Is the person I’m exchanging with the right person or not? Is he American or just lives in America? What’s his background? What is his field of expertise? Today’s social networks offer a wealth of information that could be used to better know the person you’re dealing with. Better, many of it is available for free and is only a few clicks away. Yet, many Chinese professionals don’t look up the name of their customers online to find out more about them and their businesses. It’s always better to know something rather than not know it. A few years ago, I remembered spending

在医院里抱着刚出生的宝宝。那时我才知道她刚生了孩子且正在休产假。

领英网永远是我的第一选择，因为通过领英网的资料，我可以了解我谈话对象的具体工作职责，甚至他的同事是谁，他的经理是谁，他正在做的项目，他的爱好以及他的影响力等。所有这些有价值的信息都能让交易变得更为顺畅，因为这些信息能将谈话引向共同兴趣，同时能避开那些可能会造成分歧的话题。

提示 7: 不要畏惧打电话

在销售与谈判研讨会上，我几乎总能在销售人员那儿听到这样的问题："之前有个外国买家向我要我们公司的产品目录和价格表，我们给他们发送了电子邮件但却没有收到任何反馈，我们后来一直给他们发邮件，他们从来都不回复。我们应该怎么办？应该停止联系他们吗？"如果这样的事发生在我身上，在假定对方忽略我的消息之前，我会先问问自己我联系的那个人是否还在那家公司上班，他是否换了工作。人们在离职后一般不会每一位联系人都通知。不过有一件几乎可以确定的事是他们往往会更新自己的社交媒体资料，一般来说领英网上的信息反映了他们的职位变迁。在网上做一次快速的搜索就能发现该名员工的动向。如果他还在同一家公司上班，那我会直接给他打电话！如果不打电话，我就永远无法拿到这笔生意。但是如果我打了，我就有可能拿下这笔生意或者至少得到一些反馈。这对我来说没什么。但是由于存在语言障碍，许多中国的销售代表对给外国客户打电话并没有足够的自信。他们只是持续不停地发电子邮件，一封接着一封。如果该买家的收件箱由于饱和而无法再接收新邮件了呢？逻辑上来说这时候你就应该直接给该买家打个电话。当有人发给我的电子邮件的签名里包含着他的电话号码时，这便意

days trying to get in touch with a customer but kept failing. I thought she was ignoring my calls and emails in purpose. So I looked her name up on LinkedIn to see if I could glean any information regarding her, but found nothing new. Then I typed her name on Facebook, and the first thing that came up was pictures of her at the hospital holding her new-born baby. I knew then that she just had a baby and was on maternity leave.

My first choice is always LinkedIn because by looking at a LinkedIn profile, you would be able to understand the exact duties of the person you're talking to, and eventually, who are his colleagues, his managers, the projects he worked on, his hobbies, his influencers...All this valuable information would help making the exchange smoother because it would help stirring the conversation towards topics of common interest, and stirring it away from topics where disagreements might eventually arise.

Pointer 7: Don't be afraid of placing that call

There is a question I hear almost all the time from salespeople during sales and negotiation workshops: "There is a foreign buyer who asked me for our catalogues and price-lists. We emailed them but did not receive any feed-back. We kept sending emails but we never heard back from the buyer. What should we do? Should we stop contacting them". If this happens to me, and before I assume I'm being ignored by the other party, I'd first ask myself if the person still works for the same company or if they have changed their job. People would often leave their job without notifying every single one of their contacts. One thing that is almost always sure is that they update their social media profiles, generally LinkedIn, to reflect their new career move. A quick online search would reveal where the person is. If the person is still working for the same company, then I would call him! If I don't call them, I will never get their business. If I call them, I might get their business or at least some sort of feed-back regarding where I stand. It seems obvious to me, but given the language barrier, many sales representatives in China don't have enough

味着那个电话号码是可以用来直接联系他的。于是我会写下我想谈的几个要点，然后就直接给他打电话。经验丰富的专业销售人员不应该在交易时缺乏信心，即使是在不精通语言的情况下。如果你的英语不太好，但是你带来的生意很不错，大家还是会听你的。

提示 8: 言出必行，行之必言

言出必行的意思是如果你总能做好承诺过的事情，大家就会重视你说的话。即使你没能兑现某个承诺也不要紧，只要你提前表示歉意（不是之后），并提交一份恢复方案进行弥补。我曾看到中东地区的商人用握手的方式完成了数额可观的交易。没有律师，也没有合同，仅仅用握手作为执行既定协议的承诺。

行之必言的意思是客户需要了解你正在做的事情以及你计划要做的事情其背后的逻辑和道理，特别是在他们身处世界的另一端，并且不太熟悉你行事方式的情况下。这也是为什么他们会在下单后因为没有得到你的反馈而感到不安，即便该订单其实正在处理。为了让他们不必猜测和担忧进程，最好告诉他们："我们今天在校准机器。我们会在明天早上开始生产。第一批货将需要 48 小时完成，然后我们会在周四开始包装。"

在生活中我们遇到过不少商人，他们非常擅长言出必行，但不幸的是他们很少行之必言。建立信任和赢得尊重的基础其实很简单：言出必行，行之必言。随着时间的推移，尊重和信任自然就会建立起来。一般来说获得客户的信任是需要很长的时间的，而失去客户的信任却往往只是由于一小步的差错。

confidence to pick up the phone and place that call to a foreign party. They instead keep sending emails, one after another. What if the buyer's email inbox is saturated and can't receive messages anymore? The logical way to go about this should be to call the buyer directly. When someone sends me an email ending with a signature that includes his direct phone number, it means that the listed phone number could be used to reach him. So I just prepare myself by writing down the points I want to discuss, and then call him right away. Seasoned sales professionals should not lack confidence when it comes to doing business, even if they don't master the language. If your English is not very good but the business deal you're bringing is good, people will listen to you anyways.

Pointer 8: Do what you say and say what you do

Do what you say in the sense that people will value your word if you always do what you promised you will do. It's fine if you can not execute a promise as long as you apologize in advance (not later on) and offer a recovery solution. I have seen businessmen in Middle-east closing substantial deals with a handshake. No lawyers, no contracts. Just a handshake as a promise to execute what has been agreed upon.

Say what you do in the sense that customers need to understand the logic behind what you are doing or planning to do, especially if they are on the other side of the world and not familiar with your way of doing things. So they would worry when they place an order and don't hear back from you as the order is being processed. Instead of letting them guess what's going on, it is always good to tell them: "We are calibrating the machine today. We will start the production tomorrow morning. The first batch would take 48 hours to complete, then we could start the packing process on Thursday."

In life we encounter several business people that are good at doing what they say, but they unfortunately would rarely say what they're doing. One of the first levels of establishing trust and building respect could be that simple: do what you say and say what you do. With time, the respect and trust will build up. As a general rule, it would take a long time to gain a customer's trust, though it only takes one wrong move to lose it.

书目介绍

乐 贸 系 列

书名	作者	定价	书号	出版时间
国家出版基金项目				
1. "质"造全球:消费品出口质量管控指南	SGS 通标标准技术服务有限公司	80.00 元	978-7-5175-0289-0	2018 年 9 月第 1 版
跟着老外学外贸系列				
1. 优势成交:老外这样做销售(第二版)	Abdelhak Benkerroum(阿道)	58.00 元	978-7-5175-0370-5	2019 年 10 月第 2 版
外贸 SOHO 系列				
1. 外贸 SOHO,你会做吗?	黄见华	30.00 元	978-7-5175-0141-1	2016 年 7 月第 1 版
跨境电商系列				
1. 跨境电商全产业链时代:政策红利下迎机遇期	曹磊 张周平	55.00 元	978-7-5175-0349-1	2019 年 5 月第 1 版
2. 外贸社交媒体营销新思维:向无效社交说 No	May(石少华)	55.00 元	978-7-5175-0270-8	2018 年 6 月第 1 版
3. 跨境电商多平台运营,你会做吗?	董振国 贾 卓	48.00 元	978-7-5175-0255-5	2018 年 1 月第 1 版
4. 跨境电商 3.0 时代——把握外贸转型时代风口	朱秋城(Mr. Harris)	55.00 元	978-7-5175-0140-4	2016 年 9 月第 1 版
5. 118 问玩转速卖通——跨境电商海外淘金全攻略	红 鱼	38.00 元	978-7-5175-0095-7	2016 年 1 月第 1 版
外贸职场高手系列				
1. 小资本做大品牌:外贸企业品牌运营	黄仁华著	58.00 元	978-7-5175-0372-9	2019 年 10 月第 1 版
2. 金牌外贸企业给新员工的内训课	Lily 主编	55.00 元	978-7-5175-0337-8	2019 年 3 月第 1 版
3. 逆境生存:JAC 写给外贸企业的转型战略	JAC	55.00 元	978-7-5175-0315-6	2018 年 11 月第 1 版
4. 外贸大牛的营与销	丹 牛	48.00 元	978-7-5175-0304-0	2018 年 10 月第 1 版
5. 向外土司学外贸 1:业务可以这样做	外土司	55.00 元	978-7-5175-0248-7	2018 年 2 月第 1 版
6. 向外土司学外贸 2:营销可以这样做	外土司	55.00 元	978-7-5175-0247-0	2018 年 2 月第 1 版
7. 阴阳鱼给外贸新人的必修课	阴阳鱼	45.00 元	978-7-5175-0230-2	2017 年 11 月第 1 版
8. JAC 写给外贸公司老板的企管书	JAC	45.00 元	978-7-5175-0225-8	2017 年 10 月第 1 版
9. 外贸大牛的术与道	丹 牛	38.00 元	978-7-5175-0163-3	2016 年 10 月第 1 版

书名	作者	定价	书号	出版时间
10. JAC 外贸谈判手记——JAC 和他的外贸故事	JAC	45.00 元	978-7-5175-0136-7	2016 年 8 月第 1 版
11. Mr. Hua 创业手记——从 0 到 1 的"华式"创业思维	华 超	45.00 元	978-7-5175-0089-6	2015 年 10 月第 1 版
12. 外贸会计上班记	谭 天	38.00 元	978-7-5175-0088-9	2015 年 10 月第 1 版
13. JAC 外贸工具书——JAC 和他的外贸故事	JAC	45.00 元	978-7-5175-0053-7	2015 年 7 月第 1 版
14. 外贸菜鸟成长记(0～3 岁)	何嘉美	35.00 元	978-7-5175-0070-4	2015 年 6 月第 1 版

外贸操作实务子系列

书名	作者	定价	书号	出版时间
1. 外贸高手客户成交技巧 2——揭秘买手思维	毅 冰	55.00 元	978-7-5175-0232-6	2018 年 1 月第 1 版
2. 外贸业务经理人手册(第三版)	陈文培	48.00 元	978-7-5175-0200-5	2017 年 6 月第 3 版
3. 外贸全流程攻略——进出口经理跟单手记(第二版)	温伟雄(马克老温)	38.00 元	978-7-5175-0197-8	2017 年 4 月第 2 版
4. 金牌外贸业务员找客户(第三版)——跨境电商时代开发客户的 9 种方法	张劲松	40.00 元	978-7-5175-0098-8	2016 年 1 月第 3 版
5. 实用外贸技巧助你轻松拿订单(第二版)	王陶(波锅涅)	30.00 元	978-7-5175-0072-8	2015 年 7 月第 2 版
6. 出口营销实战(第三版)	黄泰山	45.00 元	978-7-80165-932-3	2013 年 1 月第 3 版
7. 外贸实务疑难解惑 220 例	张浩清	38.00 元	978-7-80165-853-1	2012 年 1 月第 1 版
8. 外贸高手客户成交技巧	毅 冰	35.00 元	978-7-80165-841-8	2012 年 1 月第 1 版
9. 报检七日通	徐荣才 朱瑾瑜	22.00 元	978-7-80165-715-2	2010 年 8 月第 1 版
10. 外贸实用工具手册	本书编委会	32.00 元	978-7-80165-558-5	2009 年 1 月第 1 版
11. 快乐外贸七讲	朱芷萱	22.00 元	978-7-80165-373-4	2009 年 1 月第 1 版
12. 外贸七日通(最新修订版)	黄海涛(深海鱿鱼)	22.00 元	978-7-80165-397-0	2008 年 8 月第 3 版

出口风险管理子系列

书名	作者	定价	书号	出版时间
1. 轻松应对出口法律风险	韩宝庆	39.80 元	978-7-80165-822-7	2011 年 9 月第 1 版
2. 出口风险管理实务(第二版)	冯 斌	48.00 元	978-7-80165-725-1	2010 年 4 月第 2 版
3. 50 种出口风险防范	王新华 陈丹凤	35.00 元	978-7-80165-647-6	2009 年 8 月第 1 版

外贸单证操作子系列

书名	作者	定价	书号	出版时间
1. 跟单信用证一本通(第二版)	何源	48.00 元	978-7-5175-0249-4	2018 年 9 月第 2 版
2. 外贸单证经理的成长日记(第二版)	曹顺祥	40.00 元	978-7-5175-0130-5	2016 年 6 月第 2 版
3. 信用证审单有问有答 280 例	李一平 徐珺	37.00 元	978-7-80165-761-9	2010 年 8 月第 1 版
4. 外贸单证解惑 280 例	龚玉和 齐朝阳	38.00 元	978-7-80165-638-4	2009 年 7 月第 1 版
5. 信用证 6 小时教程	黄海涛(深海鱿鱼)	25.00 元	978-7-80165-624-7	2009 年 4 月第 2 版
6. 跟单高手教你做跟单	汪 德	32.00 元	978-7-80165-623-0	2009 年 4 月第 1 版

书名	作者	定价	书号	出版时间
福步外贸高手子系列				
1. 外贸技巧与邮件实战(第二版)	刘　云	38.00 元	978-7-5175-0221-0	2017 年 8 月第 2 版
2. 外贸电邮营销实战——小小开发信　订单滚滚来(第二版)	薄如骢	45.00 元	978-7-5175-0126-8	2016 年 5 月第 2 版
3. 巧用外贸邮件拿订单	刘　裕	45.00 元	978-7-80165-966-8	2013 年 8 月第 1 版
国际物流操作子系列				
1. 货代高手教你做货代——优秀货代笔记(第二版)	何银星	33.00 元	978-7-5175-0003-2	2014 年 2 月第 2 版
2. 国际物流操作风险防范——技巧·案例分析	孙家庆	32.00 元	978-7-80165-577-6	2009 年 4 月第 1 版
通关实务子系列				
1. 外贸企业轻松应对海关估价	熊　斌　赖　芸　王卫宁	35.00 元	978-7-80165-895-1	2012 年 9 月第 1 版
2. 报关实务一本通(第二版)	苏州工业园区海关	35.00 元	978-7-80165-889-0	2012 年 8 月第 2 版
3. 如何通过原产地证尽享关税优惠	南京出入境检验检疫局	50.00 元	978-7-80165-614-8	2009 年 4 月第 3 版
彻底搞懂子系列				
1. 彻底搞懂信用证(第三版)	王腾　曹红波	55.00 元	978-7-5175-0264-7	2018 年 5 月第 3 版
2. 彻底搞懂关税(第二版)	孙金彦	43.00 元	978-7-5175-0172-5	2017 年 1 月第 2 版
3. 彻底搞懂提单(第二版)	张敏　张鹏飞	38.00 元	978-7-5175-0164-0	2016 年 12 月第 2 版
4. 彻底搞懂中国自由贸易区优惠	刘德标　祖月	34.00 元	978-7-80165-762-6	2010 年 8 月第 1 版
5. 彻底搞懂贸易术语	陈　岩	33.00 元	978-7-80165-719-0	2010 年 2 月第 1 版
6. 彻底搞懂海运航线	唐丽敏	25.00 元	978-7-80165-644-5	2009 年 7 月第 1 版
外贸英语实战子系列				
1. 十天搞定外贸函电(白金版)	毅　冰	69.00 元	978-7-5175-0347-7	2019 年 4 月第 2 版
2. 让外贸邮件说话——读懂客户心理的分析术	蔡泽民(Chris)	38.00 元	978-7-5175-0167-1	2016 年 12 月第 1 版
3. 外贸高手的口语秘籍	李　凤	35.00 元	978-7-80165-838-8	2012 年 2 月第 1 版
4. 外贸英语函电实战	梁金水	25.00 元	978-7-80165-705-3	2010 年 1 月第 1 版
5. 外贸英语口语一本通	刘新法	29.00 元	978-7-80165-537-0	2008 年 8 月第 1 版
外贸谈判子系列				
1. 外贸英语谈判实战(第二版)	王慧　仲颖	38.00 元	978-7-5175-0111-4	2016 年 3 月第 2 版

书名	作者	定价	书号	出版时间
2. 外贸谈判策略与技巧	赵立民	26.00 元	978-7-80165-645-2	2009 年 7 月第 1 版
国际商务往来子系列				
国际商务礼仪大讲堂	李嘉珊	26.00 元	978-7-80165-640-7	2009 年 12 月第 1 版
贸易展会子系列				
外贸参展全攻略——如何有效参加 B2B 贸易商展(第三版)	钟景松	38.00 元	978-7-5175-0076-6	2015 年 8 月第 3 版
区域市场开发子系列				
中东市场开发实战	刘军　沈一强	28.00 元	978-7-80165-650-6	2009 年 9 月第 1 版
加工贸易操作子系列				
1. 加工贸易实务操作与技巧	熊　斌	35.00 元	978-7-80165-809-8	2011 年 4 月第 1 版
2. 加工贸易达人速成——操作案例与技巧	陈秋霞	28.00 元	978-7-80165-891-3	2012 年 7 月第 1 版
乐税子系列				
1. 外贸企业免抵退税实务——经验 · 技巧分享	徐玉树　罗玉芳	45.00 元	978-7-5175-0135-0	2016 年 6 月第 1 版
2. 外贸会计账务处理实务——经验 · 技巧分享	徐玉树	38.00 元	978-7-80165-958-3	2013 年 8 月第 1 版
3. 生产企业免抵退税实务——经验 · 技巧分享(第二版)	徐玉树	42.00 元	978-7-80165-936-1	2013 年 2 月第 2 版
4. 外贸企业出口退(免)税常见错误解析 100 例	周朝勇	49.80 元	978-7-80165-933-0	2013 年 2 月第 1 版
5. 生产企业出口退(免)税常见错误解析 115 例	周朝勇	49.80 元	978-7-80165-901-9	2013 年 1 月第 1 版
6. 外汇核销指南	陈文培等	22.00 元	978-7-80165-824-1	2011 年 8 月第 1 版
7. 外贸企业出口退税操作手册	中国出口退税咨询网	42.00 元	978-7-80165-818-0	2011 年 5 月第 1 版
8. 生产企业免抵退税从入门到精通	中国出口退税咨询网	98.00 元	978-7-80165-695-7	2010 年 1 月第 1 版
9. 出口涉税会计实务精要(《外贸会计实务精要》第二版)	龙博客工作室	32.00 元	978-7-80165-660-5	2009 年 9 月第 2 版
专业报告子系列				
1. 国际工程风险管理	张　燎	1980.00 元	978-7-80165-708-4	2010 年 1 月第 1 版
2. 涉外型企业海关事务风险管理报告	《涉外型企业海关事务风险管理报告》研究小组	1980.00 元	978-7-80165-666-7	2009 年 10 月第 1 版
外贸企业管理子系列				
1. 外贸经理人的 MBA	毅　冰	55.00 元	978-7-5175-0305-7	2018 年 10 月第 1 版

书名	作者	定价	书号	出版时间
2. 小企业做大外贸的制胜法则——职业外贸经理人带队伍手记	胡伟锋	35.00元	978-7-5175-0071-1	2015年7月第1版
3. 小企业做大外贸的四项修炼	胡伟锋	26.00元	978-7-80165-673-5	2010年1月第1版

国际贸易金融子系列

书名	作者	定价	书号	出版时间
1. 国际结算单证热点疑义相与析	天九湾贸易金融研究汇	55.00元	978-7-5175-0292-0	2018年9月第1版
2. 国际结算与贸易融资实务(第二版)	李华根	55.00元	978-7-5175-0252-4	2018年3月第1版
3. 信用证风险防范与纠纷处理技巧	李道金	45.00元	978-7-5175-0079-7	2015年10月第1版
4. 国际贸易金融服务全程通(第二版)	郭党怀 张丽君 张贝	43.00元	978-7-80165-864-7	2012年1月第2版
5. 国际结算与贸易融资实务	李华根	42.00元	978-7-80165-847-0	2011年12月第1版

毅冰谈外贸子系列

书名	作者	定价	书号	出版时间
毅冰私房英语书——七天秀出外贸口语	毅　冰	35.00元	978-7-80165-965-1	2013年9月第1版

“创新型”跨境电商实训教材

书名	作者	定价	书号	出版时间
跨境电子商务概论与实践	冯晓宁	48.00元	978-7-5175-0313-2	2019年1月第1版

“实用型”报关与国际货运专业教材

书名	作者	定价	书号	出版时间
1. 国际货运代理操作实务(第二版)	杨鹏强	48.00元	978-7-5175-0364-4	2019年8月第2版
2. 集装箱班轮运输与管理实务	林益松	48.00元	978-7-5175-0339-2	2019年3月第1版
3. 航空货运代理实务(第二版)	杨鹏强	55.00元	978-7-5175-0336-1	2019年1月第2版
4. 进出口商品归类实务(第三版)	林　青	48.00元	978-7-5175-0251-7	2018年3月第3版
5. e时代报关实务	王　云	40.00元	978-7-5175-0142-8	2016年6月第1版
6. 供应链管理实务	张远昌	48.00元	978-7-5175-0051-3	2015年4月第1版
7. 电子口岸实务(第二版)	林青	35.00元	978-7-5175-0027-8	2014年6月第2版
8. 报检实务(第二版)	孔德民	38.00元	978-7-80165-999-6	2014年3月第2版
9. 现代关税实务(第二版)	李　齐	35.00元	978-7-80165-862-3	2012年1月第2版
10. 国际贸易单证实务(第二版)	丁行政	45.00元	978-7-80165-855-5	2012年1月第2版
11. 报关实务(第三版)	杨鹏强	45.00元	978-7-80165-825-8	2011年9月第3版
12. 海关概论(第二版)	王意家	36.00元	978-7-80165-805-0	2011年4月第2版

书名	作者	定价	书号	出版时间

“精讲型”国际贸易核心课程教材

书名	作者	定价	书号	出版时间
1. 国际贸易实务精讲(第七版)	田运银	49.50 元	978-7-5175-0260-9	2018 年 4 月第 7 版
2. 国际货运代理实务精讲(第二版)	杨占林 汤 兴 官敏发	48.00 元	978-7-5175-0147-3	2016 年 8 月第 2 版
3. 海关法教程(第三版)	刘达芳	45.00 元	978-7-5175-0113-8	2016 年 4 月第 3 版
4. 国际电子商务实务精讲(第二版)	冯晓宁	45.00 元	978-7-5175-0092-6	2016 年 3 月第 2 版
5. 国际贸易单证精讲(第四版)	田运银	45.00 元	978-7-5175-0058-2	2015 年 6 月第 4 版
6. 国际贸易操作实训精讲(第二版)	田运银 胡少甫 史 理 朱东红	48.00 元	978-7-5175-0052-0	2015 年 2 月第 2 版
7. 进出口商品归类实务精讲	倪淑如 倪 波 田运银	48.00 元	978-7-5175-0016-2	2014 年 7 月第 1 版
8. 外贸单证实训精讲	龚玉和 齐朝阳	42.00 元	978-7-80165-937-8	2013 年 4 月第 1 版
9. 外贸英语函电实务精讲	傅龙海	42.00 元	978-7-80165-935-4	2013 年 2 月第 1 版
10. 国际结算实务精讲	庄乐梅 李 菁	49.80 元	978-7-80165-929-3	2013 年 1 月第 1 版
11. 报关实务精讲	孔德民	48.00 元	978-7-80165-886-9	2012 年 6 月第 1 版
12. 国际商务谈判实务精讲	王 慧 唐力忻	26.00 元	978-7-80165-826-5	2011 年 9 月第 1 版
13. 国际会展实务精讲	王重和	38.00 元	978-7-80165-807-4	2011 年 5 月第 1 版
14. 国际贸易实务疑难解答	田运银	20.00 元	978-7-80165-718-3	2010 年 9 月第 1 版

“实用型”国际贸易课程教材

书名	作者	定价	书号	出版时间
1. 外贸跟单实务(第二版)	罗 艳	48.00 元	978-7-5175-0338-5	2019 年 1 月第 2 版
2. 海关报关实务	倪淑如 倪 波	48.00 元	978-7-5175-0150-3	2016 年 9 月第 1 版
3. 国际金融实务	李 齐 唐晓林	48.00 元	978-7-5175-0134-3	2016 年 6 月第 1 版
4. 国际贸易实务	丁行政 罗艳	48.00 元	978-7-80165-962-0	2013 年 8 月第 1 版

中小企业财会实务操作系列丛书

书名	作者	定价	书号	出版时间
1. 做顶尖成本会计应知应会 150 问(第二版)	张 胜	48.00 元	978-7-5175-0275-3	2018 年 6 月第 2 版
2. 小企业会计疑难解惑 300 例	刘华 刘方周	39.80 元	978-7-80165-845-6	2012 年 1 月第 1 版
3. 会计实务操作一本通	吴虹雁	35.00 元	978-7-80165-751-0	2010 年 8 月第 1 版